Understanding
THEOLOGY
in 15 Minutes a Day

Books by Daryl Aaron

Understanding Your Bible in 15 Minutes a Day
Understanding Theology in 15 Minutes a Day

Understanding
THEOLOGY
in 15 Minutes a Day

DARYL AARON

BETHANY HOUSE PUBLISHERS
a division of Baker Publishing Group
Minneapolis, Minnesota

Published by Bethany House Publishers
11400 Hampshire Avenue South
Bloomington, Minnesota 55438
www.bethanyhouse.com

Bethany House Publishers is a division of
Baker Publishing Group, Grand Rapids, Michigan

Printed in the United States of America

Library of Congress Cataloging-in-Publication Data
Aaron, Daryl.
    Understanding theology in 15 minutes a day : how can I know God? How can Jesus be both God and man? What will heaven be like? and many more / Daryl Aaron.
        p.   cm.
    Includes bibliographical references.
    Summary: "Theology professor and former pastor presents concise overview of 40 theological concepts for lay readers"—Provided by publisher.
    ISBN 978-0-7642-1012-9 (pbk. : alk. paper)
    1. Theology, Doctrinal—Popular works. I. Title. II. Title: Understanding theology in fifteen minutes a day.
BT77.A17 2012
230—dc23   2012013961

Cover design by Eric Walljasper

12   13   14   15   16   17   18   7   6   5   4   3   2   1

This book is dedicated to
my wife, Marilyn,
and
my daughter, Kimberly,
two of God's most gracious gifts to me.

Contents

Introduction

God gave the prophet Jeremiah a research project:

> Cross over to the coasts of Kittim and look,
> send to Kedar and observe closely;
> see if there has ever been anything like this:
> Has a nation ever changed its gods?
> (Yet they are not gods at all.)
> Jeremiah 2:10–11 NIV1984

In other words, "Jeremiah, see if you can find an example of a pagan people who has traded in one god or gods for another god or gods." The implication was that he would come up with nothing. God then contrasts this discovery with the condition of Israel:

> But my people have exchanged their Glory
> for worthless idols.
>
> v. 11

That is, "The ones who belong to the one true God, the *only* God ('their Glory'), have done what not even pagans do—traded me in for *nothing* gods."

The cosmic result of that tragic reality:

> Be appalled at this, O heavens,
> and shudder with great horror,
> declares the LORD.
>
> v. 12

The reason:

> My people have committed two sins:
> They have forsaken me,
> the spring of living water,
> and have dug their own cisterns,
> broken cisterns that cannot hold water.
>
> v. 13

Stunningly, his people preferred smelly, stale, stagnant water from a leaky artificial hole in the ground to cool, fresh, pure water from an inexhaustible, divinely given source.

This text is getting at the travesty of desiring anything other than the best, our Glory, God himself. This is why, for our own well-being, we are told: "Delight yourself in the LORD" (Psalm 37:4) and "Rejoice in the Lord always" (Philippians 4:4). This is why David said:

> One thing I ask of the LORD,
> this only do I seek:
> that I may dwell in the house of the LORD
> all the days of my life,
> to gaze on the beauty of the LORD
> and to seek him in his temple.
>
> Psalm 27:4

This is why Jesus said, "The kingdom of heaven [God's dwelling] is like treasure hidden in a field. When a man found it, he hid it again, and then in his joy went and sold all he had and bought that field" (Matthew 13:44).

God himself is the greatest treasure imaginable, and theology, the study of God, is the greatest treasure hunt imaginable.

This book is about theology, but specifically about systematic theology, a branch of studies generally organized into the following categories:

Bibliology is the study of how God has made himself known generally and the Bible specifically.

Theology proper[1] is the study of God himself—who he is and what he has done and will do.

Angelology is the study of other spiritual beings—angels, demons, and Satan.

Anthropology is the study of the pinnacle of God's creation—humans, the bearers of his image.

Hamartiology is the study of that which is contrary to God—sin.

Christology is the study of the Son of God, the second person of the Trinity—who he is and what he has done and will do.

Pneumatology is the study of the Holy Spirit, the third person of the Trinity—who he is and what he has done and will do.

Soteriology is the study of God's solution to the problem of sin—salvation.

Ecclesiology is the study of the church, the body of Christ—saved people corporately.

Eschatology is the study of "last things"—what God will do in the future as he has revealed it in Scripture.

A few notes about chapter order: In a sense, theology proper could come first since everything flows from God, including the Word of God, the Bible. Normally, however, Bibliology precedes theology proper because the Bible is the primary (though not only) source of information about God. So first we must understand what it is and have confidence in what we find there. After an introduction to theology (chapter 1), Bibliology will be covered in chapters 2–5. Theology proper will follow in chapters 6–11.

Angelology (chapter 12) and anthropology (chapters 13–14) come next, since they deal with beings created by God. Hamartiology (chapters 15–16) naturally follows anthropology, since sin is now a given with regard to human nature and experience. We cannot understand humanity in the present apart from understanding its fallenness.

Christology (chapters 17–22) would fit immediately after theology proper, since Christ is God, the second person of the Trinity. However, I will cover it after anthropology and hamartiology because, in addition to being God, Jesus Christ, also fully human, became human in order to solve the problem of sin. Theology proper, anthropology, and hamartiology help us to better understand Christology.

Pneumatology (chapters 23–25) could also immediately follow theology proper, since the Spirit is God, the third person of the Trinity, but it also follows the study of the Trinity's second person. Soteriology (chapters 26–32) fits next; the work of Jesus Christ provides the basis for salvation, and the Holy Spirit applies the work of Christ to those who believe in him.

Ecclesiology (chapters 33–36) follows as it deals with the corporate nature of all believers. And eschatology (chapters 37–40) comes last because it deals with "last things."

I have written this book from an evangelical perspective. This means I am convinced of and committed to certain basic ideas: For instance, the Bible is what it claims to be—the very Word of God, without error, completely true and trustworthy; Jesus

Christ is who he claimed to be—fully and eternally God as well as fully human; Jesus really did die historically and physically, really was resurrected historically and physically, and really is coming back to earth physically and visibly; and finally, faith in Christ is the only way for us sinners to be accepted by God and enjoy his presence forever.

As we examine and discuss these issues, I will provide evidence for why they are worthy of belief. I will quote or cite biblical texts along the way, and while I could include many more, I encourage you to look up related texts and read them for yourself as well. After all, anything I might say that is not backed up by and does not adequately reflect God's Word is of little value.

Even those who share this same evangelical perspective do not all agree on everything, especially in the realm of theology. So I have included and have tried to fairly represent theological views I do not hold myself. I have also tried to keep my theological opinions from showing (too much).

It is my earnest desire that this book will whet your appetite for knowing God better, and that it will assist in laying a foundation for your personal, ongoing, lifelong pursuit of more and more of God, the supreme and priceless treasure.

Your life will never be the same. Happy hunting!

What Is Theology?

M any people, after hearing the word *theology*, roll their eyes and envision esoteric scholarly debates that have little if any bearing on real life. However, theology is much more basic, more foundational, than this, and it has everything to do with real life. The word itself comes from the Greek terms for "God" (*theos*) and "word," "thought," or "reason" (*logos*). So *theology* means: "that which can be said or thought about God—essentially, the study of God." If the primary (though not exclusive) source of information about God is the Bible, theology can be thought of as the study of the Bible: What does it teach? What is true, according to Scripture?

A more formal definition might be something like this: "Theology simply means thinking about God and expressing those thoughts in some way."[1] Notice that this describes activity. Theology is not primarily *something*, but rather the *doing* of something, specifically, thinking and expressing. The term *doctrine* refers to the results of the thinking and the content of the expressing (though sometimes *theology* is used as a synonym for *doctrine*).

Furthermore, notice from the definition that theology is not simply a mental activity; it also involves communication. This is noteworthy because knowledge of God is too essential to keep to oneself. It needs to be passed on to help others understand God as well.

If this is what theology is, then it follows that theology is something *everyone* does, for everybody thinks and talks about God to some degree. Even atheists do; they just do so in negative terms. At some level, all people are theologians, whether they know it or not.[2] The question, then, is not whether one is "doing" theology but whether one is doing theology correctly.

So *how* do we do theology correctly?

How to Do Theology

First, one truth that Christians have long understood may initially seem counterintuitive: *We must do theology in faith.* Normally we would assume that after we thoroughly understand something, we decide whether or not we should believe it. But the Bible teaches another order. The apostle Paul says:

> The person without the Spirit [the unbeliever] does not accept the things that come from the Spirit of God [e.g., God's Word, the Bible] . . . and cannot understand them because they are discerned only through the Spirit.
>
> 1 Corinthians 2:14

In other words, only a person of faith—one who trusts in God and trusts in his Word—can truly understand his Word as he intends. Anselm of Canterbury (1033–1109) put it this way: "I believe in order that I may understand." Or, as others have rephrased it, theology is "faith seeking understanding." The belief, or faith, is to precede the understanding.

This does not mean faith is blind. It is not mindless or irrational. God will never ask us to trust in something for which there is insufficient basis for belief. It does mean we must do theology in dependence upon God, the subject of our study and author of our primary truth source—the Bible, his Word. Through his Spirit, he will guide us into all truth (John 16:13).

Second, *we must do theology in humility.* This should be obvious by the very fact that God is an infinite and perfectly holy being, while we are trying to comprehend him with finite minds that have been affected by sin. (See Jeremiah 17:9, where "heart" refers to the mind.)

> "My thoughts are not your thoughts,
> neither are your ways my ways,"
>   declares the LORD.
> "As the heavens are higher than the earth,
> so are my ways higher than your ways
> and my thoughts than your thoughts."
>   Isaiah 55:8–9

So we should do theology humbly, realizing we will fall short of perfection. This also implies that we should constantly be doing theology in order to be refining it so that more and more it purely reflects the truth.

Third, *we must do theology with the right motives.* Too often theology has been motivated by pride that seeks to show the superiority of one's intellect and knowledge. This, of course, is the opposite of doing it humbly. In contrast, God-pleasing motives include doing theology to magnify him—"Whatever you do, do it all for the glory of God" (1 Corinthians 10:31)—and to help others—"Everything must be done so that the church may be built up" (1 Corinthians 14:26; see also Ephesians 4:15–16; Colossians 1:28).

Fourth, *we must do theology in the right way*. For instance, let's say the subject of our pursuit is "What does it mean to be human?" Foremost, we must regard God's Word as our primary source (more on other sources in chapter 2). Then we identify the biblical texts relevant to the topic. Next, we interpret those texts carefully, in order to understand them accurately, seeking to determine what the authors intended to communicate to the original audiences (on biblical authorship and related matters, see chapters 3–5). Finally, we synthesize our findings in order to answer, "What does the entire Bible teach about what it means to be human?"

How to Understand Theology

Theology is also a more expansive term for a number of sub-disciplines (including, for example, biblical theology, historical theology, and natural theology). Again, this book's approach falls under the category of *systematic* theology: the study of the Bible that attempts to categorize or systematize its teaching according to broad topics. Generally, ten categories are represented: What does the Bible teach about the Bible? God? Jesus Christ? the Holy Spirit? angels? humans? sin? salvation? the church? the future (or last things)?

The answers are hardly irrelevant or stuff to interest only academic types. They are thoroughly useful, profoundly applicable, even vital to our overall well-being. Paul demonstrated this by how he organized his letters. The first part, generally theological, explains *what* his readers should know and believe (e.g., Romans 1–11; Ephesians 1–3). The latter part, generally practical, applies the theology and illustrates *how* his readers should live as a result of their faith and knowledge (e.g., Romans 12–16; Ephesians 4–6).

The order is crucial: *Theology (biblical truth) is the basis for Christian living.* Paul also showed its relevance by repeatedly encouraging pastors (in his pastoral epistles: 1 and 2 Timothy, Titus) to teach people "sound doctrine." The word *sound* means "healthy." The point is that biblical truth is necessary, for without it we will be unhealthy spiritually and vulnerable to false teaching (a serious concern of Paul in these letters).

While this relevance and applicability of theology is not always readily apparent, we ought to assume that it *is* relevant and continue to ponder God-revealed truth, with God's help, as increasingly we better grasp its relevance. God does *not* waste his words on trivialities. Theology based on the Word of God should not only affect our thinking (what we believe and understand) but also our behavior (how we live), and ultimately our character (who we are).

Therefore, and finally, to do theology correctly *we must apply it to our own lives and help others apply it to their lives.* God desires to use theology (biblical truth) to transform us into godly people. It is my prayer that he will work through the following chapters to continue doing just that.

INTERESTING FACT

Up until the last couple of centuries, theology was known as the "queen of the sciences." The assumption was that since everything comes from God, nothing can be sufficiently understood apart from God. Therefore, you were not considered to be educated in *any* field of study unless you had also studied theology. Oh, for the good old days, when theology was given its appropriate and necessary place!

How Can I Know God?

We can know God for one reason only: God has made himself known. If God had not chosen to do this, we could not have known him. That is, God is not accessible through our senses, our reason, our experience, or any other means apart from his willingness to be accessible. Our knowledge of God is absolutely dependent upon divine revelation; and not only is he *willing* to be known, he *desires* to be known.

The term *revelation* comes from the Greek word *apocalupsis* (also the title of the New Testament's last book), which means an "uncovering" or "revealing" of something that was previously unknown. The doctrine of revelation, then, means we can know God because he has chosen to make himself and his works known.

There are two kinds of divine revelation: general and specific.

General Revelation

General revelation refers to knowledge of God that is available to all people of all times and all places. Such knowledge comes in three ways.

First, *general revelation comes through nature,* that is, through what God has made. Psalm 19:1 says, "The heavens declare the glory of God; the skies proclaim the work of his hands." God communicates through his creation. Paul writes, "Since the creation of the world God's invisible qualities—his eternal power and divine nature—have been clearly seen, being understood from what has been made, so that people are without excuse" (Romans 1:20). Some of God's nature can be "clearly seen" through his works. This is not just communication but *clear* communication, which is why "people are without excuse." Everyone should see the degree to which God is revealed through nature.

Second, *general revelation comes through human beings,* that is, those who bear God's image. This would include, for one thing, a sense of the divine. In the verse before Paul's statement about what can be known of God in nature, he says, "What may be known about God is plain to them, because God has made it plain to them" (Romans 1:19). God has placed within all humans an inner sense of his existence, and he has made this plain.

All humans have a sense of the eternal as well. Ecclesiastes 3:11 says, "He has also set eternity in the human heart." This means we all have a God-given inner sense that there is more than just the here-and-now; there is an eternal realm—God's realm.

As Paul shows, all humans also have a God-implanted sense of morality:

When Gentiles, who do not have the [written] law, do by nature things required by the law, they are a law for themselves, even though they do not have the law. They show that the requirements of the law are written on their hearts, their consciences also bearing witness, and their thoughts sometimes accusing them and at other times even defending them.

Romans 2:14–15

This moral sense is the human conscience, a reflection of God, who himself is the moral standard. He has written his laws on our hearts.

Third, *general revelation comes through history*, that is, how God works in time and space. This is what Daniel had in mind when he said that God "changes times and seasons; he deposes kings and raises up others" (Daniel 2:21; see also Job 12:23; Acts 17:26). History is the working out of God's plans and purposes, and whether we know it or not, we experience and observe his work in all current events.

So through at least these ways—nature, humans, and history—God has made himself known to all people. Everyone everywhere knows that the one true God exists and knows something about him. As Paul makes clear, all people are accountable for this knowledge ("without excuse," Romans 1:20), but tragically, all "suppress the truth by their wickedness" (Romans 1:18).

Specific (Special) Revelation

Whereas general revelation is available to all people generally, specific (or special) revelation is only available to specific people and at specific times and places. Historically, this has taken many forms, such as the following:

First, God has revealed himself *through an audible voice*. This seems implied in Genesis 12:1: "The Lord had said to Abram. . . ." A clear example is when God called out to Samuel (see 1 Samuel 3), and at first Samuel thought Eli was calling him.

Second, God has revealed himself *through dreams*, such as Joseph's (Genesis 37:5–11). Later, Pharaoh had two related dreams and God enabled Joseph to interpret them (Genesis 41:1–37). Joseph specifically told Pharaoh, "God has revealed to Pharaoh what he is about to do" (vv. 25, 28).

Third, God has revealed himself *through visions*, for instance, to Abraham (Genesis 15:1). The book of Daniel contains four visions God gave him regarding future world rulers, kingdoms, and God's work to establish his eternal kingdom that would replace all human kingdoms (Daniel 7–12).

Fourth, God has revealed himself *through messengers*, such as prophets and angels. The Hebrew word translated *prophet* (*nabi*) means "speaker," that is, one who speaks for God. The Hebrew and Greek terms translated *angel* (*malak* and *angelos*) both mean "messenger." Sometimes angels accompanied a vision God gave to a prophet (e.g., Zechariah 1:9; 2:3).

Fifth, God's ultimate revelation of himself was *through his Son, Jesus Christ*. This began even before the incarnation, that is, before he permanently took on a human nature in addition to his eternal divine nature. For example, the Old Testament often references the "angel of the LORD (*Yahweh*)," as in Judges 6:11, when this specific "angel" came to Gideon while he was threshing wheat. In the same passage, this individual is referred to only as "the LORD" (v. 14), so clearly this is not just any angel of God but God himself. Most scholars believe this specifically is the second person of the Trinity appearing on earth as a human. The term applied is *theophany*, an appearance or visible "manifestation" (Greek *phainō*—to become visible, to appear) of "God" (Greek *theos*).

This ultimate revelation became permanent when Jesus was born. The apostle John shows the significance by referring to him as the "Word" (*logos*)—"The Word was God" (John 1:1), and "The Word became flesh and made his dwelling among us" (v. 14). As a result, he "has made [God] known" (v. 18). Jesus Christ is the supreme communication from God and of God. We can know God because he became one of us in the person of Jesus Christ.

Essentially, for us today, specific revelation is the written Word of God, the Bible. In the Gospels we have the record of the ultimate revelation, Jesus Christ. We also have the records of

God's own voice, of dreams, of visions, of prophets and angels, and so much more. The Bible—what it says about itself and the implications of this—will be the focus of chapters 3–5.

SOBERING FACT

While general revelation is sufficient to make all people guilty of turning away from God (Romans 1:18-20), it is not sufficient to provide salvation for anyone. Only specific revelation—specifically, Jesus Christ and the gospel—are sufficient for salvation (Romans 10:13-17).

How Do We Know the Bible Is the Word of God?

In chapter 2 we saw that God's specific or special revelation to us is the Bible. This is the primary (though not exclusive) source for what we know about God and the various subjects of theology. So it is absolutely vital that we understand what the Bible claims about itself, and the implications that follow.[1]

Christians refer to the Bible as the Word of God, but why? One of the main reasons we know this is true is that it makes this claim for itself. Is the assertion invalid because Scripture makes it? Not necessarily. And there is a lot of supporting evidence.

There is extra-biblical ("outside the Bible") evidence that the Bible is God's Word. For example, prophecies recorded in Scripture happened in history. The Messiah's birth was foretold to be in Bethlehem (Micah 5:2); the birth of Jesus fulfilled that prophecy. Isaiah mentioned the name of a Persian king, Cyrus, more than 150 years before he reigned (Isaiah 44:28; 45:1). Daniel

11 is an amazingly detailed prophecy of a series of Greek kings who reigned between the Old and New Testament periods. Who knows the future well enough to reveal it before it happens? Only God. Archaeological finds also contribute to the Bible's claim. For example, though some biblical critics had claimed there was no King Belshazzar in Babylon (see Daniel 5), archaeology has confirmed his existence. Many such external evidences confirm that the Bible is what it claims to be.[2]

Inspiration

The most straightforward claim within the Bible itself is the foundation of Christian belief in its "inspiration." The first phrase of 2 Timothy 3:16 says, as the *New International Version* renders it, "All Scripture is God-breathed." Some versions, such as the *New American Standard Bible*, translate this as "All Scripture is inspired by God." But the NIV wording is quite literal. The Greek word, which precisely means "God-breathed," is found only here in the New Testament, so possibly Paul coined this term to convey exactly what he wanted us to understand about the nature of Scripture.

The first implication is that the Bible begins with God, as is true of all divine revelation. He is the ultimate source of what is written in it. Another implication comes from the imagery of "breathing out," namely, speaking or communicating. The Bible finds its source in God and is the result of his having willed to communicate with people.

Another important text regarding the doctrine of inspiration is 2 Peter 1:20–21, which speaks of the process God used to communicate his written Word. Verse 20 says, "Above all, you must understand that no prophecy of Scripture came about by the prophet's own interpretation." The Greek word rendered *interpretation* is used only here in the New Testament and is challenging to translate. In light of verse 21 (below), it seems a better sense of what Peter is saying is as follows: "No prophecy of Scripture ever comes about by the prophet's own *imagination*"[3] (NET).

Peter's concern here is with the origin of Scripture, and in verse 20 he rules out the prophets—the Bible's human authors were *not* its ultimate source. And verse 21 provides the denial's explanation: "For prophecy never had its origin in the human will, but prophets, though human, spoke from God as they were carried along by the Holy Spirit." The first phrase is Peter's restatement that the Bible did not come about by its human authors deciding on their own what they wrote. The *New Living Translation* puts it this way: "Above all, you must realize that no prophecy in Scripture ever came from the prophet's own understanding, or from human initiative. No, those prophets were moved by the Holy Spirit, and they spoke from God."

The origin of Scripture, once again revealed to be God himself, is to be understood first and foremost as an act of his will. Having determined to communicate (reveal), he did so through the agency of his Holy Spirit, the Bible's divine author, who caused its human authors to write what they wrote.

Based on these texts regarding the nature of Scripture, the Christian doctrine of biblical inspiration can be summarized something like this: God took the initiative in choosing to communicate; he did so through the work of the Spirit, who in turn empowered the human authors. The result is that what the human authors wrote was in every sense the Word of God. So the doctrine of inspiration emphasizes that God is the ultimate author but also affirms the human writers as authors. This is called the *dual authorship* of Scripture. The Bible is primarily God's Word but also legitimately the words of the various human authors.

Theories of Inspiration

Down through the centuries since the New Testament books were completed and added to the Old Testament, many have claimed to believe in biblical inspiration under definitions that differ to some degree from what the Bible says on the matter. The following are "defective ideas of inspiration":

Verbal dictation, or *mechanical inspiration*, is the view that God fully dictated the Bible, and that the human authors merely wrote down what he told them to record, basically reducing them to word processors with a heartbeat.

There is some truth in this. For example, Moses wrote down the Law as God instructed, and maybe some prophetic messages were received from God word-for-word. But if he dictated the entire Bible, there would be one style of writing—God's—and this is not what we observe. Each human author has a different style.

The apostles Paul and John, for instance, had very distinct styles, including favorite vocabulary and ways of "packaging" what they wrote. So most of the Bible does not fit with divine dictation. Rather, God normally worked through the human authors' intellects, experiences, and manners of expression in such a way that what they wrote was exactly what he intended. There is mystery here in terms of how this worked, even as the implication is clear that the words the authors chose were the exact words God intended.

Dynamic inspiration is the view that the ideas or concepts are divinely inspired but not the very words used to express those concepts. That is to say, God made sure the human writers accurately communicated his ideas, but he gave them complete freedom to express those ideas through whatever words they selected.

There certainly is truth here also. Scripture's ideas and concepts most definitely are inspired. However, the Bible itself (e.g.,

Jeremiah 23:30–36; 26:12–15) claims that the very original *words* the human authors used were the ones God intended.

Human intuition is the view that the Bible is not God's Word at all, just great human literature that reflects human intuition and insight into the human condition. This notion is attractive because this is exactly how, in English, we often use *inspired*, *inspiring*, and *inspirational*. It is common to hear someone comment on how "inspiring" a pastor's sermon was, or how "inspired" a poet was when she wrote a certain poem, or how "inspirational" a Bach composition is. These comments usually imply that the pastor, poet, or composer has produced something remarkable and meaningful, an excellent *human* work of literature or art. Specifically, this understanding of Scripture is reflected in a more liberal Christian view of the Bible.

The obvious problem, however, is that this would drain the supernatural dimension from the Bible, and it contradicts explicit internal claims. Again, 2 Timothy 3:16 pointedly says the biblical "writing" (the literal meaning of the Greek word translated *Scripture*) is inspired, not the writers themselves.

Due to these deviations from the historic understanding of inspiration, evangelical theologians now tend to refer to the *verbal, plenary* inspiration of Scripture. *Verbal* clarifies that not only the Bible's ideas but also its very initial words (Hebrew and Greek) are from God. *Plenary* clarifies that not just some but all of its words are from God.

INTERESTING FACT

The opening verses of Deuteronomy contain an intriguing interplay that illustrates the Bible's dual authorship: "These are *the words*

Moses spoke to all Israel. . . . *Moses proclaimed* to the Israelites all that *the* LORD *had commanded* him. . . . *Moses began to expound* this law, saying: '*The* LORD *our God said* to us at Horeb . . .'" (1:1–6). Deuteronomy indeed accords with the words of Moses but also and primarily is the Word of God.

What Are the Implications of the Bible Being the Word of God?

If the Bible is in fact God's Word, then there are very important implications we must consider. Scripture itself presents some of these implications. The following are just a few.[1]

The Bible Is True

Because God is always truthful and correct in whatever he says (2 Samuel 7:28; Titus 1:2; Hebrews 6:18), his Word also is truthful and correct in whatever it says (Psalm 12:6; Proverbs 30:5). Jesus said to his Father, "Your word is truth" (John 17:17). He does not just say God's Word is true but rather equates it with truth itself—ultimate Truth. Theologically, this is to say that the Bible is *inerrant*, that is, without error.

Jesus' own understanding of this can be seen in John 10. When he claimed deity for himself, saying, "I and the Father are one" (v. 30), the Jews picked up stones to execute him for blasphemy. Jesus then said,

> Is it not written in your Law, "I have said you are gods"? If he called them "gods," to whom the word of God came—and the Scripture cannot be set aside—what about the one whom the Father set apart as his very own and sent into the world? Why then do you accuse me of blasphemy because I said, "I am God's Son"?
>
> vv. 34–36

Jesus said Scripture "cannot be broken" (v. 35 NASB), that is, cannot be shown to be false or wrong in any way. Furthermore, he backs up this claim on the basis of one word—*gods* (*elohim*)—in the middle of verse 6 of Psalm 82.[2] He was staking his own life on the "unbreakableness" of one word from one verse in the Hebrew Bible! If this is the nature of just one word in Scripture, how much more so the whole.

This view has been expressed by renowned Christian thinkers from early on. For example, Augustine wrote, "I firmly believe that no single error due to the [biblical] author is found in any one of [the canonical books]." Martin Luther quoted this statement in agreement and added, "The Scriptures have never erred" and "The Scripture *cannot* err."[3]

The Bible Is Trustworthy

Because God is faithful and always can be trusted to do what he says (Numbers 23:19; 1 Corinthians 1:9; 1 Thessalonians 5:24), the Bible, as the Word of God, also can be trusted (2 Samuel 7:28). The theological way of saying this is that the Bible is *infallible.* This word frequently gets used as a synonym for *inerrant,* but, more precisely, it says more by taking an additional step (based on inerrancy): Because the Bible is without error, it will never fail in its message or purpose, nor will it ever cause anyone to fail, be led into error, or be fooled into believing something unworthy of belief.

Jesus made a startling statement that reflects this idea:

> Do not think that I have come to abolish the Law or the Prophets; I have not come to abolish them but to fulfill them. For truly I tell you, until heaven and earth disappear, not the smallest letter, not the least stroke of a pen, will by any means disappear from the Law until everything is accomplished.
>
> Matthew 5:17–18

When Jesus referred to the "Law or the Prophets," he had in mind all of the Scriptures then available—what we call the Old Testament. His assertion, then, was that from those Scriptures, not the smallest letter or least pen stroke would be lost. The "smallest letter" in the language Jesus spoke was a *yodh,* or Y. It would look to us like an apostrophe ('), written at the top of a line of letters with just a flick of the wrist. The "least stroke of a pen" was a part of a letter that distinguishes it from another letter. If we start with a P and add a stroke at the bottom, we end up with an R. If we start with an I and add a stroke at the top, we end up with a T. Jesus is saying that until the end of time, God will protect and preserve his written Word down to individual words, tiny little letters, even parts of letters! He would not do this unless it were all true and trustworthy (see also Matthew 24:35).

Some evangelical theologians prefer to speak of the Bible as infallible but *not* inerrant. They mean that while the Bible is truthful and trustworthy in matters of faith and practice—that is, what Christians must believe to be saved and how they are to live—there may be errors regarding history, geography, or science.[4] This view is sometimes called "limited inerrancy," meaning inerrancy limited to areas of faith and practice.

The International Council on Biblical Inerrancy (ICBI) was founded in 1977 to defend the traditional view of the Bible's complete inerrancy. In their "Chicago Statement on Biblical Inerrancy,"[5] they replied to this view (which rejects inerrancy but affirms infallibility) as follows:

> We affirm that Scripture, having been given by divine inspiration, is infallible, so that, far from misleading us, it is true and reliable in all the matters it addresses. We deny that it is possible for the Bible to be at the same time infallible and errant in its assertions. Infallibility and inerrancy may be distinguished, but not separated.
>
> Article XI

> We deny that Biblical infallibility and inerrancy are limited to spiritual, religious, or redemptive themes, exclusive of assertions in the fields of history and science.
>
> Article XII

Indeed, it would seem that complete infallibility and complete inerrancy must necessarily go together. History has shown that when it is thought that Scripture contains even minimal errors, gradually and eventually more and more supposed "errors" are perceived, even in areas of faith and practice.

The Bible Is a Unity

Because the Bible ultimately comes from one source and mind (God's), it reflects a perfect harmony of thought. Thus it contains no contradictions, as there are no contradictions in God's mind. One portion will never contradict any other; a biblical text will always agree with and complement all others.

With typical bluntness, Luther wrote, "It is impossible that Scripture should contradict itself, only that it so appears to the senseless and obstinate hypocrites."[6] This is not to deny that the Bible will sometimes *seem* to contradict itself, but as Augustine wisely said, "When I am confronted in these Books with anything that seems to be at variance with truth, I put it down . . . to my own mistaken understanding of the passage."[7]

FUN FACT

I jokingly say that "limited inerrancy" is like me claiming "partial omniscience"—that is, I know absolutely everything, except those things I do not know. "Limited inerrancy" says there are no errors in Scripture, except where there are errors.

What Are Other Implications of the Bible Being God's Word?

So far we have seen that the Bible is inspired, meaning it is indeed God's Word. Thus other things must be true by way of implication.

One is that the Bible is inerrant. God does not make mistakes, and his Word does not include them.

Another is that the Bible is infallible. If there are no mistakes in it, then it will never fail in what it says or cause anyone to fail in believing it.

This also implies the unity of Scripture. There are no contradictions in it, just as there are no contradictions in the mind of God.

Here are a few more important implications.[1]

The Bible Is Authoritative

Because God is our final authority, the Bible is our final written authority. Because it comes from God, and God's authority is ultimate, its authority is greater than any human (pastor, priest, bishop, king, president, prime minister), human institution (church, denomination, council, senate, parliament, court), or human document (creed, catechism, confession, doctrinal statement, ordinance, law). The Bible deserves to be believed and obeyed, for to disbelieve or disobey it is to disbelieve or disobey God himself.

This is why the prophets continually called Israel to obey God's law as given in the Hebrew Scriptures. At the end of the Old Testament, God said through his prophet Malachi, "Remember the law of my servant Moses, the decrees and laws I gave him at Horeb for all Israel" (Malachi 4:4). This is what Paul meant when he wrote, "What I am writing to you is the Lord's command" (1 Corinthians 14:37). John stated the same truth while dealing with the threat of false teaching: "We are from God, and whoever knows God listens to us; but whoever is not from God does not listen to us" (1 John 4:6).

The ICBI Chicago Statement puts it this way:

> We affirm that the Holy Scriptures are to be received as the authoritative Word of God. We deny that the Scriptures receive their authority from the Church, tradition, or any other human source.
>
> Article I

> We affirm that the Scriptures are the supreme written norm by which God binds the conscience, and that the authority of the Church is subordinate to that of Scripture. We deny that Church creeds, councils, or declarations have authority greater than or equal to the authority of the Bible.
>
> Article II

I have chosen to discuss the authority of Scripture somewhat later, since it is a logical implication of revelation, inspiration, inerrancy, and infallibility. However, the ICBI dealt with biblical authority at the very beginning of their statement, likely due to its utmost importance. I also affirm this importance, especially with the multiplying "voices of authority" all around us regarding what is acceptable and what is not, what is right and what is wrong, what is good and what is bad. Christians are to embrace the absolute authority of God's Word in all that it states and are to willingly and gladly believe and obey it, even when our culture says to believe and do something different. This is not easy to do, but it is vital to please God first and honor his Word.

The Bible Is Sufficient

What we have in the Bible—Old and New Testaments—is what God intended for us to have. We are not waiting for further revelation or clarification. The Bible is sufficient in the sense that it contains all we need to know to be made right with God and live before him in a way that pleases him.

This was really true at each stage of God's progressively revealing his Word. Paul wrote to Timothy, "From infancy you have known the Holy Scriptures, which are able to make you wise for salvation through faith in Christ Jesus" (2 Timothy 3:15). The "Holy Scriptures" Paul was referring to were what we call the Old Testament. Even though the New Testament was yet to come, the Old Testament was sufficient *at that time,* until God inspired the New.

The very next thing Paul wrote was the aforementioned primary text regarding the doctrine of inspiration:

> All Scripture is God-breathed and is useful for teaching, rebuking, correcting and training in righteousness, so that the servant of God may be thoroughly equipped for every good work.

vv. 16–17

Once more, "Scripture" technically refers to our Old Testament, but Paul adds that through it, the believer "may be *thoroughly* equipped for *every* good work." That is, in the Bible (both Testaments now) we have everything we need to know to be who God wants us to be and do what God wants us to do.

This is not to say that the Bible answers all of *our* questions. Rather, it answers the questions for which God wants us to know the answers. Apart from that, our answers to other questions remain speculative and tentative. This should encourage us, however, in ensuring that all *important* questions, from God's perspective, can be answered based on what we have in his Word. Therefore, we should go there looking for these answers with the confidence that they can be found.

The Bible Is Clear

Not only is the Bible sufficient for what we are to know and do, but it is also understandable to the average reader. The theological term for this is *perspicuity* (which is *not* very clear, although that is exactly what the word means!). Psalm 19:7 says, "The statutes of the LORD are trustworthy, making wise the simple." Psalm 119:130 declares, "The unfolding of your words gives light; it gives understanding to the simple." It's encouraging that graduate training in Hebrew, Greek, and theology are not necessary to comprehend the Bible.

This does not mean everything in the Bible is easy to understand. The things of God are deep and ultimately incomprehensible. Some things we need to study extensively and ponder deeply in order to grasp them better. Neither does Scripture's clarity nullify the need for pastors and Bible professors (I like my job!). But it does mean believers should not be totally dependent upon such people for their understanding of Scripture. With a humble dependence on God, the help of the Holy Spirit (John 14:26; 16:13; 1 Corinthians 2:9–14), and an earnest desire to know truth, any reader *can* and *should* understand what God wants that reader to know, believe, and obey.

MORE FACTS

More could be said on how the Scripture's sixty-six books were included (canonicity), how it was copied and passed on to more and more people (transmission), and how it was made available to those who could not read Hebrew and Greek (translation). These factors and others add to the confidence we ought to have in the Bible, even our English translations. They are briefly addressed in Daryl Aaron, *Understanding Your Bible in 15 Minutes a Day,* chapters 21, 23-24.

What Characteristics of God Make Him Unique?

Theology that focuses on God specifically—who he is and what he has done—is known as "theology proper." This is really the most important topic in theology, because if you do not understand God properly, you cannot understand the rest of theology properly. Everything else flows from God's character and work, even what we have already looked at: God's Word.

God is an infinite being, and therefore we cannot know him perfectly and exhaustively. In this sense, God is "incomprehensible." Nevertheless, God has revealed himself—primarily through his Son, Jesus Christ—and therefore he is comprehensible to an extent (John 14:7; 1 John 5:20). Our goal, then, is to so desire to know our amazingly great God that we continue to deepen our understanding of him for the rest of our lives.

But we should also be careful to distinguish between knowing *about* God and really knowing *God*. Knowing about God just deals with facts. Really knowing God includes relationship.

Our longing should be to have such an intimate and growing relationship with God that we want to go beyond mere facts about God. This means we need to consider implications and applications of what we know about God. If God is like this, then what? What difference does it make? We will try to do a bit of this in what follows, but truly it will only be scratching the surface.

We could start with arguments for the existence of God, but that is not where the Bible starts. The biblical authors simply *assume* God's existence and build on that (Genesis 1:1), so that is what we will do as well. Arguments for the existence of God really fall more under philosophy or the philosophical end of theology.

The study of God's nature is usually done by examining his attributes or characteristics, that is, whatever God has revealed to be true about himself. Sometimes called "perfections," these are usually divided into two categories. God's *incommunicable* attributes are those characteristics that are only true of himself; they make him unique. God's *communicable* attributes are those characteristics he shares to a limited extent with humans.[1] Here and in chapter 7, we will consider a few of his incommunicable attributes. In chapter 8 we will consider a few of his communicable attributes.

Some of God's Incommunicable Attributes

A good place to start is with God's *spirituality*. This seems to be the closest we can come to "defining" the nature of God. Jesus said, "God is spirit, and his worshipers must worship in spirit and in truth" (John 4:24 NIV1984). This basically means he is immaterial or incorporeal—he has no physical, material body. The second commandment is related to this fact: "You shall not make for yourself an image in the form of anything in heaven above or on the earth beneath or in the waters below"

(Exodus 20:4). Trying to represent the one, true God by means of a material form fundamentally misrepresents him. God's spiritual nature also means that he is invisible; he cannot be seen by the human eye (1 Timothy 1:17; 6:15–16).

One application of God's spirituality comes from that declaration of Jesus: Because "God is spirit," we are to worship him "*in spirit* and in truth" (John 4:24). At the least, this means we must not try to drag him into our material realm, as if he could be contained in a place—cathedral, church, chapel, wherever. Rather, *we* enter into *his* realm—the spiritual—and we can do that anywhere, at any time.

Another application is that God's realm is ultimate and central, and our prerogatives in life should reflect this. That's what Jesus meant when he said, "Seek first his kingdom and his righteousness [spiritual things], and all these things [material things] will be given to you as well" (Matthew 6:33).

Another important implication of God's spirituality, a divine attribute in itself, is his perfect *unity* or *simplicity*. This means God has no parts to divide up. Nothing can be added to God, and nothing can be taken away from God. As we study his attributes, we should not think of them as "parts," that if we add all his attributes together the sum will be God. Rather, we should think of his attributes as different perspectives on, or descriptions of, his perfect unity.

God's *sovereignty* means he rules over and controls his entire creation absolutely and completely. The Bible often uses terms like *reign*, *authority*, and *dominion* to describe this. Read King David's prayer in 1 Chronicles 29:10–16, where, even though he does not use the word *sovereignty*, the concept permeates what he says. Sovereignty is why Paul can say that God "works out everything in conformity with the purpose of his will" (Ephesians 1:11). What God wants to do, God does (see also Psalm 115:3).

Because he is God, he does not tolerate encroachments upon his sovereignty. We must always be humble before him and gladly willing to submit to him. The story of King Nebuchadnezzar, recorded in Daniel 4, is an illustration (especially vv. 25, 34–37). Another application is that we can trust the work of God implicitly. He is in perfect control of all circumstances of our lives, even when those circumstances *seem* to us to be totally out of control.

An implication of God's sovereignty, and yet another attribute, is his *self-sufficiency* or *independence* (Acts 17:24–25). God needs nothing from outside of himself; he is not dependent on anyone or anything *for* anything. In contrast, all the rest of creation is totally dependent upon him.

God's *omnipotence* means he is able to do whatever he wills to do; he is not limited by anything outside of himself; he is all-powerful. This does not mean that God can do *anything*—he cannot do anything contrary to his nature. For example, he cannot sin or cause himself to cease to exist.

It does mean he can do anything that is consistent with his nature and his will. This is why God can simply say, "Let there be," and what did not exist before springs into existence (Psalm 33:6, 9). This is why he could enable Abraham's wife, Sarah, to conceive at the age of eighty-nine (Genesis 18:10–14). This is why he could enable Mary to conceive Jesus apart from a human father (Luke 1:26–38). And this is why he can save sinners (Matthew 19:23–26). After all, the gospel "is the power of God that brings salvation to everyone who believes" (Romans 1:16).

This assures us that God will do whatever he promises to do (Romans 4:20–21). It also assures us that when we need help and strength, God can and will provide it (Ephesians 1:18–20).

God's *omnipresence* means he is present everywhere (Psalm 139:7–10). This along with his omnipotence and sovereignty is a source of great comfort to believers (Psalm 139:10). Over and over again, when God's people needed comfort and encouragement, he would say, "I will be with you" (Exodus 3:11–12; cf. Deuteronomy 31:7–8; Joshua 1:9; Hebrews 13:5–6; et al.). On the other hand, God's omnipresence is a warning: Those who persist in sin cannot hide themselves or their sinful deeds from him (Psalm 139:11–12).

FACT?

As I delight to tell my students at the beginning of the term, theology class is not just for a semester; it will be for all eternity. Here is my proof: Question—How long does it take to comprehend something that is infinite, that is, God? Answer—An infinite number of days, that is, eternity. Every day of eternity, I think, we will learn something new and amazing about God. I can't wait!

What Other Characteristics of God Make Him Unique?

In addition to being all-powerful and everywhere-present, God is all-knowing, an attribute known as *omniscience*. This means he has perfect and eternal knowledge of all things (Psalm 139:1–6; Isaiah 40:12–14; 1 John 3:2). He cannot learn anything because he has always known everything. He also knows all things that could have happened but did not. An interesting biblical illustration is in 1 Samuel 23:10–13, where God tells David what would happen *if* King Saul came to a certain city looking for David. As it turns out, Saul never came and those things never happened. God knows what would have happened if . . . (you had married so-and-so!).

Another implication of omniscience seems to be that God knows everything past, present, and future. Recently there has been theological debate about the future aspect of his knowledge. "Open theology" is convinced that God does not know the future *exhaustively*—some of the future is "open," unknown even to him. This position is held by some Arminians who believe that if God knows the future, then the choices we will make in the future are not *free* choices, which would be troublesome to the importance they place on human free will. Most Arminians and all Calvinists do not share this concern, believing that God's exhaustive knowledge of the future is not at odds with human freedom.[1]

Closely connected to omniscience is God's *wisdom*,[2] which refers to God's ability to choose the best goals and the best possible means to those goals in order to determine the best overall plan for all that he does. Knowledge has to do with information; wisdom has to do with how that information is used—it is practical, not just cerebral. God knows all things and also knows how to use perfect knowledge in the best way.

The best and highest goal God has chosen is to glorify himself (Numbers 14:21–23; Isaiah 48:11; Romans 11:36; Philippians 2:10–11).[3] One of the very best means toward this goal is how God has created: "How many are your works, LORD! In wisdom you made them all" (Psalm 104:24; see also Proverbs 3:19). Another means to God's glory is how he has made salvation available for all. After reflecting on the riches of his grace through Jesus Christ, resulting in justification by faith, which Paul had just unpacked (Romans 3–11), he wrote, "Oh, the depth of the riches of the wisdom and knowledge of God! . . . To him be the glory forever! Amen" (Romans 11:33, 36; see also Ephesians 1:3–12).

By way of application, if the best goal God could choose was his own glory, we cannot improve on this. So we too should make it our goal to glorify God through good works (Matthew 5:16), bearing fruit (John 15:8), and by everything that we do (1 Corinthians 10:31). Also, if God knows everything perfectly, including ourselves and our needs, and if his wisdom is perfect (and he is sovereign and omnipotent), we can trust him implicitly. He always does what is the very best for us (Romans 8:28).

Another incommunicable attribute of God is his *immutability*. This means he never changes in his essence or nature. James 1:17 says, "Every good and perfect gift is from above, coming down from the Father of the heavenly lights, who does not change like shifting shadows." Hebrews 13:8 says of Jesus, the Son of God, he "is the same yesterday and today and forever" (see also Malachi 3:6).

This is a part of what makes God unique. Every aspect of his creation is characterized by constant change of some sort—growth, decay, expansion, contraction. God alone experiences no change like this.

Any change regarding God is in relation to what is outside of him. For example, sinners are under his wrath, but when sinners repent, they are under his blessing. What happened to the city of Nineveh as recorded in the book of Jonah is a good example of this.

An amazing application is that we enjoy in our relationship with God something that we do not have in any other relationship—stability and predictability (from God's end). In every other relationship, we are never exactly sure what is going on within the other person; every such bond carries with it a degree of uncertainty and risk. Not so with God. We always know he loves us (Romans 8:38–39), has forgiven us (Colossians 2:13), and is with us to guide us and protect us; he will never abandon us (Matthew 28:20)!

Another attribute of God is his *holiness*. God is sinless, morally perfect, totally apart from evil (Job 34:10; Habakkuk 1:12–13).[4] Even further, he is the very standard of moral perfection. Numerous times in Scripture, God says, "Be holy, because I am holy" (Leviticus 11:44; 19:2; 1 Peter 1:15–16). All laws and commands that come from God flow from and reflect his holy nature.

However, we still have not gotten to the most basic meaning of God's holiness, which is that he is distinct from everyone and everything else. God is unique, in a category all by himself. This is expressed in Exodus 15:11, "Who among the gods is like you, LORD? Who is like you—majestic in holiness?" The answer: No one. Similarly, 1 Samuel 2:2 says, "There is no one holy like the LORD; there is no one besides you; there is no Rock like our God." One effect this should have upon us is what it had on Isaiah. After having a vision of God and hearing angels say, "Holy, holy, holy is the LORD Almighty" (Isaiah 6:3), he was humble, repentant, and willing to serve God however he could. An understanding of God's holiness will revolutionize one's life.

INTERESTING FACT

The concept of God's *glory* is probably best seen not as an attribute but rather the effect of all of God's attributes when they are revealed. John Piper says it well: "God's glory is the beauty of his manifold perfections. . . . It can refer to the infinite moral excellence of his character."[5] Read the account of Moses asking God to show his glory. God did, but had to "tone it down" for Moses to survive the experience of a lifetime (Exodus 22:18–34:9).

What Characteristics of Himself Does God Share With Humans?

Even the characteristics of himself that God shares with humans—communicable attributes—are not quite the same in us. All of these are perfect in God but imperfect in people. Nevertheless, it is with regard to these attributes that we as humans can most relate to God.

Justice/Righteousness

Closely related to God's holiness is his *justice* or *righteousness*. Both English words are used to translate the Hebrew and Greek terms that are biblically applied to this aspect of God's being, and while they share a moral sense, there are other nuances as well.

First, a person is said to be "righteous" if he personally conforms to moral standards, that is, obeys laws. In this sense, God's righteousness is essentially the same as the moral aspect of his holiness (see chapter 7). God perfectly conforms to the moral laws that reflect his nature in the first place.

Second, a person is said to be "just" if he rightly applies moral standards to other people and situations. This is the job of judges, whom we all hope are just. Considering this specific facet of God's being, the meaning of his righteousness/justice is that he requires all morally responsible creatures to conform to his own perfect morality, and he judges accordingly if they do or do not—he rewards the righteous and punishes the unrighteous. God, the judge of the universe, is always a just judge (Genesis 18:25; Deuteronomy 32:4; Psalm 51:4; Revelation 16:5–7). And this is at least reflected in us all, for we have a built-in sense of right and wrong and long for justice. Even very young children are known to say, "That's not fair!"

It isn't unusual for God himself to be charged with unfairness. The prophet Habakkuk struggled with God's justice when he thought God was overlooking the sin of his people and also when God told him he would use a pagan nation to punish his sinful people (Habakkuk 1:3–4, 12–13). Job struggled with God's justice for allowing him, a righteous man, to suffer extensively (Job 9:14–22).

Most of us feel this way at times, when something God is doing (or not doing) strikes us as being unjust. Those are the times when we must remember that no matter what we're thinking or how we're feeling, God *is* just. He knows everything we do not know and has wisdom we lack. We must trust him always, and never more so than when we struggle. That is exactly the point of Habakkuk (3:17–19) and Job (42:1–6).

We're also to keep in mind that a day is coming when God will render perfect and eternal justice (Acts 17:31; 2 Thessalonians 1:5–8); let us be content to wait for that (Isaiah 30:18). We must also remember that God calls us to be just as well. We are to treat all people with equal fairness (Isaiah 1:17; Amos 5:24; Micah 6:8).

Love

"God is *love*" (1 John 4:8, 16), and so he acts in love. The exodus is the great Old Testament symbol of this; because of God's love, he redeemed his people from enslavement in Egypt (Deuteronomy 7:7–8; Hosea 11:1). The cross is the great New Testament symbol; because of God's love, he sent his own Son to die for sinful people (John 3:16; Romans 5:8; Galatians 2:20).

What does love mean? Here is a generally accepted definition: Love always does what is best for the object of love, regardless of the cost. If you really love someone, you will *desire* the best for them, and to the extent that you can, you will *do* what is best for them—even when they may not think it is best and even when it may require self-giving and even sacrifice.

Love was what motivated God to send Jesus Christ to die for our sin so that we could have what is best—God himself! He paid the highest price for our well-being. Many of us grew up singing, "Jesus loves me; this I know," so we can easily take God's love for granted. But we should battle against this. In fact, we should be stunned by the very thought that *God loved us* so *much* that he gave his only Son to bear his wrath in our place.

God rightly expects us to love and obey him because he loved us first (John 15:15; Romans 5:8). He wants us to channel his love to others (Matthew 22:39; John 13:34–35), even to the extent of dying for them (1 John 3:16) and even when they are enemies (Luke 6:27–35).

Mercy and Grace

Closely related to God's love is his *mercy* and *grace*, which really are two sides of the same coin. God's mercy means he is good to those who are suffering, even when that suffering is the result of their own sin. Biblical words such as *compassion*, *longsuffering*, and *kindness* illustrate this point (Exodus 34:6–7;

Psalm 103:8–11; Luke 1:77–78; Philippians 2:27). Another way of describing God's mercy is that he does *not* give us what we *do* deserve. Though we all deserve to suffer because we are sinful people, God, in his mercy, helps us patiently, kindly, and compassionately. It's clear to see that his mercy is closely related to his love for us.

God's grace refers to his goodness toward those who ought to experience his judgment, that is, he *does* give us what we do *not* deserve. "Unmerited favor" or "blessing" is a shorthand definition. Again, we do not deserve—we have not earned—anything good from God. But because he is gracious, he gives us his goodness (Romans 3:24; Ephesians 1:6–7; Titus 2:11). This is why we receive salvation through Christ totally apart from anything we do (Romans 3:27–28; 11:6; Ephesians 2:8–9; Titus 3:5–7).

As with God's love, we must never take for granted God's mercy and grace demonstrated through Jesus Christ. When we remember we are sinners who deserve punishment and can do nothing to impress God, that he is just, owes us nothing, and ought to give us what we deserve—eternal death—grace becomes truly amazing.

Not only are we saved by grace but we also live as saved people through God's grace by the power of his Holy Spirit within us. This is one of the themes of Paul's letter to the Galatians, who, even though they knew they had been saved by grace, had been duped into thinking that the rest was up to them (e.g., Galatians 3:1–6; 5:4, 16–18). The point is our lives as Christians are totally dependent upon God's grace from beginning to end. This also means that just as God has shown us mercy and grace, so should we treat others in the same way. We should care for others in need and do what we can to alleviate their suffering. We should treat others better than they deserve to be treated, even those who have mistreated us.

INTERESTING FACT

Another aspect of God's love for the righteous is his discipline. The writer of Hebrews (12:5-6) quotes Proverbs: "My son, do not make light of the Lord's discipline, and do not lose heart when he rebukes you, because the Lord disciplines the one he loves, and chastens everyone he accepts as his son." While discipline is not enjoyable initially, God does it for our good because it brings about greater holiness (vv. 10-11). That is what love does.

What Does It Mean That God Is a Trinity?

One of the many realities that makes Christianity unique is the doctrine of the Trinity, which Christians have maintained since the first century, long before it was stated in creedal form in the fourth century. The earliest believers certainly did not understand it based on a significant depth of reflection—that took a while—and though it is not succinctly stated in any one verse, it is the clear and unavoidable implication of many biblical texts.

Simply stated, the doctrine of the Trinity is that God is one in essence (or being, or nature) and three in person, each of the three persons fully and eternally sharing in the one divine essence. This would be a logical contradiction if the doctrine were affirming that God is one and three in the same way at the same time. However, the affirmation is that God is one in one aspect (essence) and three in a different aspect (person).

Contrary to what some think, the Trinity is not an intriguing yet impractical theological oddity; rather, it is absolutely integral to the Christian faith, as we will see. The doctrine is not irrational, but it is beyond the perfect comprehension of us humans; it does involve mystery. This should not overly concern us, for God himself is beyond our perfect comprehension.

Scripture Teaches the Trinity

Both Testaments are clear: There is *one* true God. Judaism is renowned for being strictly monotheistic; Deuteronomy 6:4 states, "Hear, O Israel: The LORD our God, the LORD is one" (see also Psalm 86:8–10; Isaiah 45:14; 46:9). The New Testament does not deviate. For example, "There is one God and one mediator between God and mankind, the man Christ Jesus" (1 Timothy 2:5; see also 1 Corinthians 8:4–6; Ephesians 4:6; James 2:19).

Regarding the threeness of God, the Old Testament is less clear but includes strong hints. For instance, there are plural personal pronouns, such as in Genesis 1:26: "Then God said, "Let *us* make mankind in *our* image, in *our* likeness" (see also Genesis 3:22; 11:7; Isaiah 6:8). Other texts, like Isaiah 61:1, make distinction between the divine persons: "The Spirit [the Holy Spirit] of the Sovereign LORD [the Father] is on me [the Son of God or Messiah], because the LORD has anointed me to proclaim good news to the poor" (see also Isaiah 48:16; 63:9–10).

The divine threeness is revealed more clearly in the New Testament. There are texts that affirm Jesus as God and the Spirit as God, with the Father (more on this in later chapters). There are texts that mention all three persons together, the most well-known being the Great Commission: "Go and make disciples of all nations, baptizing them in the name of the Father and of the Son and of the Holy Spirit" (Matthew 28:19; see also 2 Corinthians 13:14; Ephesians 4:4–6). Interestingly, the word *name* is in the singular, even though three persons are "named." There are also events when all three persons are present or involved, as at Jesus' baptism, when the Father speaks from heaven, referring to Jesus as his Son, and the Spirit descends upon Jesus as a dove (Matthew 3:16–17), and in Jesus' prayer, when he, the Son, asks the Father to send the Spirit (John 14:16–17).

Errors Regarding the Trinity

Some have gone wrong in their efforts to make the nature of God understandable. For example, some Christians have believed—and some people have accused all Christians of believing—in three *gods*; that is an error called tritheism. However, the biblical doctrine of the Trinity is that there is only one true God, not three.

Other Christians have believed that there is one God while denying that God is three persons. Rather, they say, the one God reveals himself in different ways, or modes, at different times: Sometimes he is the Father, sometimes the Son, and sometimes the Holy Spirit, but not all three at the same time. This mistake, called modalism, would solve the mystery but does not adequately account for events where all three persons are present and involved at the same time (as mentioned above).

Arianism, another attempt to "solve" the Trinity, is named after Arius (c. 250–336), who taught that the Father is eternal God, and he created the Son, who in turn created the Spirit. This is also known as subordinationism, for it implies that the Son is subordinate/inferior to the Father and that the Spirit is subordinate/inferior to the Father and the Son. Arianism, which holds that the Son and the Spirit are not *fully* God, was condemned as heresy in AD 325.

Orthodox Statement of the Doctrine of the Trinity

Due to misunderstandings such as these, in the fourth century the early church developed what is known as the Nicene Creed:

I believe in one God, the Father Almighty, Maker of heaven and earth, and of all things visible and invisible. And in one Lord Jesus Christ, the only-begotten Son of God, begotten of the Father before all worlds; God of God, Light of Light, very God of very God; begotten, not made, being of one substance with the Father, by whom all things were made. . . . And I believe in the Holy Spirit, the Lord and Giver of Life; who proceeds from the Father and the Son; who with the Father and Son together is worshiped and glorified. . . .

Implications of the Trinity

The Trinitarian nature of God is vitally important and should have significant impact on our lives. Here are a few suggestions.

First, authentic worship is at stake. God has revealed himself as Trinitarian. Since true worshipers must worship God in spirit and in *truth* (John 4:23–24), we cannot truly worship him apart from regarding him as he is, even if we do not perfectly comprehend what that means.

Second, an all-sufficient basis for salvation for all who will believe is at stake. The need was for a sacrifice of infinite value to pay for the many sins of many people. If Jesus is anything less than fully and eternally God, his limitations would prevent him from fully accomplishing the work of salvation.

Third, healthy personal relationships with the Father, with the Son, and with the Spirit are at stake. To the degree that we do not accept and embrace the fullness of God as he has revealed himself, we will be unable to develop meaningful intimacy with God the Father, God the Son, and God the Holy Spirit.

Fourth, healthy personal relationships between believers are at stake. Christian relationships are to be modeled after and reflect the perfect unity and love that exist between the three persons of the Trinity. Jesus prayed "that all of [my followers] may be one, Father, just as you are in me and I am in you. . . . that they may be one as we are one—I in them and you in me" (John

17:21–23). God is love; love has been eternally active among the Trinity's persons, infinitely before God created other beings to love. We are to reflect this in our love for one another (1 John 4:7–21), "being like-minded, having the same love, being one in spirit and of one mind" (Philippians 2:2).

The doctrine of the Trinity is a *precious* truth that should continually draw us back to contemplation of our amazing God. And it is a *practical* truth that should profoundly affect how we live as Christians.

FUN FACT

Tertullian, an early Latin-speaking theologian (c. 160–c. 225), was the first to use the term *trinitas* in discussing God's nature. He also used *persona* to refer to the diversity within the one being of God. Apparently, Tertullian coined 509 new nouns, 284 new adjectives, and 161 new verbs.[1] I guess the lesson is: If words fail, make some up.

Did God Really Make Everything?

In the last three chapters, we have been considering the person of God—who he is. In this chapter and the next, we will be considering the work of God—first his work of creation, and then his work of providence.

God created everything—this fact utterly permeates Scripture! That the biblical writers brought it up over and over again establishes its importance. And the implications for one's worldview are enormous, as we will see.

What does the Bible teach about God's work of creation? The main account is in Genesis 1 and 2, and though opinions differ regarding proper interpretation of some details—it is *not* an easy text to understand in detail—some aspects are crystal clear.

The Power of God in Creation

For one, God demonstrated his mind-boggling power to speak everything into being: "God said, 'Let there be . . .'"

(Genesis 1:3, 6, 9, 11, 14, 20, 24, 26; see also Psalm 33:6; Hebrews 11:3). Speaking is an expression of thought or, in this case, will. God could have simply *thought* everything into existence.

Only God is eternal; *everything* else came about through his will (Isaiah 44:24; John 1:3). This includes both the material and spiritual realms (e.g., angels; Colossians 1:16). The theological term (from Latin) for such creation is *ex nihilo*, meaning "out of nothing." God did not use already-existing raw matter (as we do); he brought the material into being, and he formed it.

One implication of note is that God is ultimate reality. That fact rules out a worldview or philosophy known as dualism, which asserts that there are two ultimate realities—for example, spirit and matter. There is nothing higher or of greater value than God, and there is nothing or no one equal to God. He and he alone is worthy of worship.

Further, reflecting his matchless wisdom (Psalm 104:24; Proverbs 3:19), God created in the very best way he could have created. Thus Genesis 1 states over and over, "God saw that it was good" (vv. 4, 10, 12, 18, 21, 25) and finally, "it was very good" (v. 31). Out of the nearly infinite number of different possibilities, he chose the one very best way to create; he could not have improved on what he did in any way.

This is important because it means that evil is not inherent to creation. That rules out another form of dualism, i.e., that good and evil are opposing ultimate realities. Evil did invade God's perfect creation, and early on, but it is not eternal.

Also, that God's original creation was good in and of itself means that he can make it so again. His handiwork will be perfected through his redemptive or re-creative work, by which he will reverse and remove the effects of evil and sin and restore creation to what he originally intended.

The Purpose of God in Creation

God's purpose in creation is also clear. He made everything for his glory (Psalm 19:1; Isaiah 43:7; Revelation 4:11), and in this sense *all* creation is first and foremost *theocentric*—about God. But it is likewise proper to say he made everything for humans, for us to live and thrive (Genesis 1:27–30). Our environment provides air to breathe, water to drink, food to eat; planet earth is precisely the right distance from the sun for a life-conducive temperature range (though we in Minnesota sometimes wonder about this in the winter).

That God created this world for humans is also implied by the fact that Adam and Eve are the pinnacle of his creation. People were his "last act" of creation. In a secondary sense, then, creation is *anthropocentric*—for humans.

This *all* implies meaning and purpose in the existence of everything. This *all* is no convenient "accident"; there is a divine reason for what God made, for what *is*. And once more, even sin cannot keep him from fulfilling his purposes—in the world as a whole or through humanity in particular.

What Creation Reveals

What can we learn about God from the doctrine of creation? As already noted, the Creator is an astoundingly *powerful and wise* God who loves people, and in his goodness has provided for them through what he has made. So he is a *personal and relational* God who desires closeness to humans. By the way, we should not imagine that he created people because he was lonely. The doctrine of the Trinity reveals perfect eternal love between its three persons. Rather, God created in order to share his *loving goodness*, which we experience primarily through relationship.

We see God's *sovereignty* in what he has made. The principle is that you are sovereign over what you create (e.g., copyright and patent laws). Therefore, because God created everything, he is sovereign over everything and has the right to rule over it.

We see God's *transcendence*, which refers to his being outside of and over his creation; he is not contained within it. Yet he is not *only* outside and over, he also is down here and very much involved from moment to moment. This is referred to as God's *immanence*, and we must regard these realities in balance. God is not either/or but both/and. If we so emphasize transcendence that immanence is lost, we arrive at deism—the idea that the Creator God is now off doing other things, no longer involved with what he created. If we so emphasize immanence that transcendence is lost, we arrive at pantheism—the notion that God is so involved in creation that Creator and creation are one and the same; creation is God and God is creation.

What can we learn about creation from the doctrine of creation? Again, that there is meaning and purpose in all God has made—especially human existence. In addition, everyone and everything is totally dependent upon God for existence itself. We are not self-sufficient—we are radically God-dependent, even for our very next breath. This means we are to look to him and trust him for what we need in every dimension of life.

There is also God-given responsibility for humans as the pinnacle of his creation. First, we were created to bear God's image, so we are accountable to reflect his nature (Genesis 1:26–27). Second, we are tasked with caring for the rest of creation (Genesis 1:28). We will come back to this in chapter 13, regarding the doctrine of humanity.

INTERESTING FACT

Many scientists deny the Creator God. Ironically, however, their work is dependent upon an implication of his creation: It is rational and ordered; it makes sense; it works according to nature's laws, which are also God's creations and reflect his nature. If creation were not like this, the scientific method itself would not work.

How Does God Work in the World?

The Bible teaches that, having created the universe, God continues to be at work in it. He does not abandon it or leave it to operate on its own; rather, he continues to be intimately and actively involved. This is generally known as the doctrine of *divine providence*, which, more specifically, is regularly described by means of three related ideas.

Dimensions of Divine Providence

First, God sovereignly rules and controls his creation (Psalm 47; Daniel 4:17): the doctrine of *divine governance* or *guidance* (also referred to as God's sovereign will or sovereign decrees). God had a plan for his creation even before he had created anything, and everything he does is for the purpose of working out that plan (Acts 2:23; 4:28; Ephesians 1:4, 11). His highest purpose in every act is to glorify himself (Isaiah 48:11; Ephesians 1:6, 12, 14). As supremely sovereign and omnipotent, what he has determined to accomplish, he will accomplish (Job 42:2; Isaiah 14:24–27; 46:10–11; Romans 8:28) as he guides his creation and history to fulfill his designs.

Second, God preserves in existence what he has called into existence (Acts 17:28; Colossians 1:17; Hebrews 1:3): the doctrine of *preservation*. The implication is that if God did not do this, what he had created would simply cease to exist (Job 34:14–15). Not only did God create everything through his unequalled power, he also sustains everything through that same power.

Third, God works through his creation in order to carry out his plans: the doctrine of *concurrence* (meaning that God works in harmony, cooperation, or agreement with creation). For example, he controls weather, and through it, he provides rain that then nourishes vegetation, animals, and people (Psalm 135:7; 104:14; 147:8–18; Matthew 5:45). He also works through people and events in history (Daniel 2:21; Jonah 1:15; 2:3; Acts 4:27–28; 17:26).

Up to this point, all evangelical theologians would agree. However, answers differ to questions such as these: *How* does God govern the world? To what *extent* does he control people and the events of history?

Two classical theological systems need to be introduced at this point: Calvinism and Arminianism. These agree in most areas but disagree on a few very significant matters, namely, providence and predestination (which is really a subcategory of providence; back to this in chapter 27).

Briefly stated, Calvinists believe that God meticulously controls his creation down to the details. Arminians believe that God controls in a more general way that allows for genuine human free will. Lately, this issue has been thought of in terms of "divine risk." Calvinism maintains *no risk;* God accomplishes his will perfectly and completely. Arminianism holds that God takes a *risk* in the sense that he allows humans to act contrary to his will, such that his will may not be perfectly accomplished. By the way, the ideas behind both belief systems were around long before the theologians they are named after.

Calvinism on Sovereignty and Free Will

Calvinism, named after the French Protestant reformer John Calvin (1509–1564), follows in the tradition of Augustine in emphasizing God's sovereignty and therefore his complete control over all things. Calvinists affirm that humans make genuine free choices but in a way that is compatible with God's total sovereignty. (This is the *compatibilism* view of human free will.) True divine sovereignty and true human freedom are not mutually exclusive, hard as this may be to understand (which Calvinists acknowledge). They are *both* biblical concepts, so they must be compatible.

This view centers on the scriptural portrait of God as *all*-powerful, reigning over *everything,* doing "*whatever* pleases him" (Psalm 135:6). Paul says he "works out *everything* in conformity with the purpose of his will" (Ephesians 1:11). Calvinists emphasize that *everything* means "everything." Thus God, who is holy and is never responsible for evil, nevertheless is in control of "accidents" (e.g., see Job 1:21; 42:11), "catastrophes" (e.g., see Isaiah 45:7; Amos 3:6), and "coincidences" (e.g., see Proverbs 16:3), even controlling and working through evil and sin for his purposes (Genesis 50:20; Exodus 4:21; 7:3; 9:12; Romans 9:17 and other texts on the hardening of Pharaoh's heart; 1 Samuel 16:14; Proverbs 16:4; Isaiah 45:7; Amos 3:6).

God also determines and is in control of those who will believe in Jesus for salvation and those who will not (Romans 8:29–30; Ephesians 1:5, 11). (Again, more on predestination in chapter 27.) God is sovereign over human choices and actions (Proverbs 16:9; 21:1; John 6:44; Acts 4:27–28; 13:48).

Arminianism on Sovereignty and Free Will

Arminianism, named after another Protestant theologian, Jacob Arminius (1560–1609), came about as a reaction to the Calvinist emphasis on God's meticulous sovereignty. It affirms that God is totally sovereign and *could* control absolutely everything, but, due to his love, he willingly limits his control to guarantee that humans are free to make choices apart from divine determination, including even the choice to hate God and disobey him. (This view of free will is called *libertarianism*, i.e., humans are always free to make decisions apart from outside coercion.)

So God does not control meticulously but rather generally. He will accomplish his intent in a way that does not violate the free will he lovingly gave to the humans he created. Arminians believe that the Calvinist view of God's sovereignty necessarily violates—is incompatible with—genuine human free will; these cannot both be true. If God determined human choices, he could not hold people accountable for those decisions and judge them accordingly.

In this regard, Arminianism emphasizes the *many* biblical commands to trust (Psalm 115:9–11; Proverbs 3:5; Isaiah 26:4), love (Deuteronomy 6:5; Matthew 22:37), and obey God (Deuteronomy 6:24–25; 9:23; John 14:15, 21, 23), along with *plentiful* warnings of judgment for those who do not (Leviticus 26:14–39; 2 Thessalonians 1:8). It seems impossible to reconcile this with God's controlling human choices and actions. How can he hold people responsible for decisions *he* predetermined? Rather, these commands and others all seem to assume individual freedom to obey or disobey God.

Closely connected to this is the idea that if God really does love people, he must give them the authentic choice of loving him in return. How could sovereignly determining human "love" be satisfying to him? That would be like programming a computer to continually print out flattering things about you. Big deal!

Arminians believe that the Calvinist understanding of providence actually makes God the author or cause of sin and evil, which, obviously, would violate the Bible's teaching regarding his holiness. (As mentioned above, Calvinists disagree that their view necessitates this.) If God is truly holy, he cannot be responsible for sin in any sense, certainly not causing or using it (Job 34:10; Habakkuk 1:13; 1 John 1:5). Arminian theology stresses that evil and sin find their source in humans and angels who have freely chosen to rebel against God. He *allows* sin, but he does *not* cause or use sin.

Both Calvinists and Arminians acknowledge that these matters are challenging to comprehend. Nevertheless, they are scripturally relevant, so crucial to understanding God and life that we need to ponder them deeply—and certainly *not* avoid them.

COMFORTING FACT

Despite these difficult issues, the doctrine of God's providence ought to give us a sense of peace and trust in him as we experience life, particularly times of suffering and trouble. Nothing happens to us apart from what God controls, in some sense, and also uses for our good (Roman 8:28).

What Are Angels and Demons?

The doctrine of angels is unusual in that it deals with beings that are part of the spiritual realm, which is beyond our powers of observation. So we are entirely dependent upon what we are told about them in Scripture, as opposed to what we can learn about them through investigation. As we have seen, even though God also dwells in the spiritual realm, there is a degree to which he has made himself known through general revelation. For angels, we only know what God has told us about them.

Another reason this doctrine is unusual is that many scientists and all naturalists deny any spiritual realm and therefore the existence of spiritual beings. At the same time, recent polls show that a large percentage of the U.S. population does believe in the existence and work of angels.

Actually the Bible talks a lot about angels—over 250 times, from the very beginning to the very end (*especially* at the end, in Revelation). What does the Bible say about these beings? Like us, they are created, but like God, they are spiritual beings without physical bodies: "Are not all angels ministering spirits?"

(Hebrews 1:14). Paul, in a clear reference to evil angels, said, "Our struggle is not against flesh and blood" (Ephesians 6:12).

Apparently there are many angels. The apostle John had a glimpse into heaven and recorded, "I looked and heard the voice of many angels, numbering thousands upon thousands, and ten thousand times ten thousand" (Revelation 5:11). Many biblical texts indicate they are magnificent beings, superior in some ways to humans (2 Peter 2:11; Hebrews 2:6–7). Yet like humans, they are finite (Daniel 10:10–14). They are powerful but not all-powerful. They are intelligent but not omniscient.

Their titles seem to indicate their primary responsibility. The Hebrew word *malak* and the Greek word *angelos,* though often translated "angel," both literally mean "messenger." So one reason God originally created them was for delivering his messages (e.g., Daniel 10). Other primary activities include worshiping God (Revelation 5:8–14), carrying out his judgments (Revelation 8–11), and protecting his people (Acts 5:19; 12:7–11).

It seems that all angels were created good and holy—they are referred to as "holy ones" in Psalm 89:5–7 and "holy angels" elsewhere—but at some point, many rebelled against God. This seems to be the point of texts like 2 Peter 2:4, "God did not spare angels when they sinned, but sent them to hell," and Jude 6, "The angels who did not keep their positions of authority but abandoned their proper dwelling—these he has kept in darkness, bound with everlasting chains for judgment on the great Day." These are referred to as "evil spirits" (Luke 7:21) and often as "demons" (Romans 8:38; James 2:19), especially in the Gospels (Matthew 8:28–33; Luke 4:33–36). Paul calls them "spiritual forces of evil in the heavenly realms" (Ephesians 6:12).

The most widely known demon is *Satan* (meaning "adversary," e.g., Zechariah 3:1). The Hebrew word is used over fifty times in the Old Testament. The Greek term applied to him is *diabolos* (meaning "accuser" or "slanderer"; see Matthew

4:1; Ephesians 4:27; Revelation 12:9), from which the English word *devil* is derived. Satan leads the fallen angels who rebelled against God; he is called "the prince of demons" (Matthew 12:24; "Beelzebub" is another title for Satan); Jesus referred to "the devil and his angels" (Matthew 25:41).

Jesus referred to the result of the angelic rebellion when he said, "I saw Satan fall like lightning from heaven" (Luke 10:18). Paul seems to indicate that the rebellion was due to pride (1 Timothy 3:6); Satan apparently wanted to be in God's place. Isaiah 14:12–17 and Ezekiel 28:11–19 are two Old Testament texts that may refer to Satan and his rebellion.[1] God declares:

> You said in your heart,
> "I will ascend to the heavens;
> I will raise my throne
> above the stars of God;
> I will sit enthroned on the mount of assembly,
> on the utmost heights of Mount Zaphon.
> I will ascend above the tops of the clouds;
> I will make myself like the Most High."
>
> Isaiah 14:13–14

> Your heart became proud
> on account of your beauty. . . .
> So I threw you to the earth.
>
> Ezekiel 28:17

The activity of Satan and his army of fallen angels is generally to oppose God, to thwart his plans and his actions. One way this is done is essentially by trying to offer an "attractive alternative"—actually a counterfeit. Again, Satan wants to usurp heaven's throne, to become the alternative supreme ruler. And he appeals to human desire for the same thing. He advised that Eve disregard God's command not to eat the fruit of the Tree of Knowledge of Good and Evil (Genesis 2:17) because "God knows that when you eat from it your eyes will be opened, and *you will be like God,* knowing good and evil" (3:5).

Satan's temptations of Jesus really added up to an enticement to avoid suffering and dying as a way to receive his kingdom (Matthew 4:8–9; Luke 4:5–7). Paul says, "Satan himself masquerades as an angel of light . . . [and] his servants also masquerade as servants of righteousness" (2 Corinthians 11:14–15). Satan even offers a counterfeit messiah in the person of the Antichrist (2 Thessalonians 2:9–11).

Regarding unbelievers, demons blind their minds to the gospel (2 Corinthians 4:4; Luke 8:12) and deceive them (John 8:44; 1 Timothy 4:1). Satan is the ruler of unbelievers and of the fallen world in general (1 John 5:19).

Regarding believers, demons tempt them in order to draw them into sin (1 Corinthians 7:5; 1 Thessalonians 3:5), to accuse them of sin in order to paralyze them with guilt (Revelation 12:10), and to hinder their work in serving God (2 Corinthians 2:11; 1 Thessalonians 2:18).

What are some lessons we should learn from all of this? Positively, Christians should be encouraged by the work of good angels on their behalf, whether or not it can be perceived. (Read 2 Kings 6:8–23, especially v. 17!) Negatively, with regard to Satan and demons, we should take their threat seriously—they are still dangerous. However, we should also remember that through his death and resurrection, Jesus Christ has ultimately broken their power and sealed their eventual doom (Colossians 2:13–15; Hebrews 2:14). They will eventually be judged and thrown into the lake of fire forever (Revelation 20:9–10).

For now, we are told to resist Satan (James 4:7—note the promise: "He will flee from you"; 1 Peter 5:9) and flee temptation (1 Corinthians 6:18; 10:13). God has given us the resources we need to fight against Satan and demons—God's "armor"—but it is our responsibility to use it and take a stand against our true enemies (Ephesians 6:13–18). Our true confidence is that God is greater than Satan and demons, and he is on our side (1 John 4:4).

INTERESTING FACT

Even though angels are superior in many ways to humans, Scripture never says they bear the image of God, and, in fact, the saints (Christians) will judge angels (1 Corinthians 6:3).

What Does It Mean to Be Human?

There are many issues surrounding us these days that make it all the more vital to understand what the Bible has to say about being human. For example, evolutionary theory says there is really no fundamental difference between humans and animals; humans are just more highly evolved animals. If so, one implication might be that since humans are only animals, then human euthanasia can make sense. After all, we "put down" animals to alleviate suffering. Why not human animals?

Will exponential advancements in computers (e.g., artificial intelligence) and robotics "inspire" us to no longer distinguish between people and machines? Is a day coming when the latter will be able to do all the former can do? Do we then treat humans like instruments and appliances and devices—that is, throw them out when they don't work as well as they once did?

Made in God's Image

What can we learn from the Bible about questions like these? As we've seen, humans are created beings and therefore need to relate to the rest of creation. This means we are dependent upon God for our ongoing existence and that our purpose, like the rest of creation, is to bring glory to him (Isaiah 43:7). This purpose, then, gives our lives meaning.

We are not an accident of nature; we were intentionally and purposefully created by God. More than that, we are valuable to him. He cares so much for us that he knows the number of hairs on our head (Matthew 10:30; and he knows that for some of us that number decreases daily!).

Even though as created beings we relate to the rest of creation, we are distinct within the created order. Humans are the pinnacle of God's creation; everything else was put here for our well-being. This brings us to probably the most important thing the Bible has to say about people: We are made in the image of God (Genesis 1:26–27; 5:1; 9:6; 1 Corinthians 11:7; James 3:9). This is crucial because it seems essentially to be a biblical definition of "humanity." *To be human is to be a divine image-bearer.*

However, even though this concept is key to comprehending humanity's significance, the Bible does not explicitly clarify what it means. The texts cited above say that this is *so* but do not explain it much. A variety of explanations have been put forward.[1]

How Do We Bear God's Image?

First, the *substantive* view suggests that the image of God means humans share certain characteristics with him. So in this sense, the image has to do with something that characterizes who we are—our being. For example, God has rationality, or reason, and humans do as well (*Homo sapiens* means "thinking being"). God is a moral being as are humans; we have consciences and think in terms of right and wrong. God is relational; so are humans. This has been the main view of Christians for a long time. One weakness is that it is largely speculative, without much explicit biblical support.

Second, the *relational* view suggests that the image of God means humans experience a relationship with God primarily, and secondarily with other humans. So this view is that rather than being something we are, the image is something we have—relationships. This reflects the relationships within the Trinity.

One of the strengths of this view is that it does capture something unique about humans. Plants and animals do not and cannot have this kind of relationship with God. One weakness is seen in regard to the image and unbelievers. The Bible says that apart from Christ, all people are separated from God. That is, non-Christians have *no* relationship with him. Would this mean they also do not bear his image?

Another weakness might be that this view seems to assume something in the substantive view, namely, that humans are relational beings. We cannot have relationships without being relational. So even though this view gets at something important, it is really based on something more fundamental in our *being* as humans.

Third, the *functional* view suggests that the image of God means humans are given a function. Rather than being something we are, or something we have, the divine image is something we do. A clear strength of this view is that certain texts could be used to support it. For example, Genesis 1:26–28:

> God said, "Let us make mankind in our image, in our likeness, so that they may rule over the fish in the sea and the birds in the sky, over the livestock and all the wild animals, and over all the creatures that move along the ground."
>
> > So God created mankind in his own image,
> > in the image of God he created them;
> > male and female he created them.

God blessed them and said to them, "Be fruitful and increase in number; fill the earth and subdue it. Rule over the fish in the sea and the birds in the sky and over every living creature that moves on the ground."

The image, accordingly, is that humans rule over, fill, and subdue the earth. This passage does indicate a close connection between the image and the responsibility, yet it does not necessarily equate them. Also, this view likewise seems based on something more fundamental about the being of humans, namely, that we can do what God has told us to do because of who he made us to be—our *being*, once again.

So as we assess these views, clearly they all point out important factors about humans that set us apart from the rest of creation, but the relational and functional views seem to be based on aspects of the substantive view. The image of God, then, apparently refers to those characteristics within humans that we share with God—how our being overlaps with his being.

What It Means to Bear God's Image

What are some implications?

For one thing, even though we do share some characteristics, only God is infinite and unlimited. A fundamental part of being human is to be finite and have limitations. We will have these limitations forever. Again, this means that we always will be—and should always acknowledge that we are—dependent upon the infinite and unlimited One.

For another, since humans bear the image of God, human life is sacred (Genesis 9:6). This also has implications for any violence against unborn children and for all forms of abuse—physical, verbal, sexual, emotional. All of these violate God's image in the individual.

Furthermore, since *all* humans bear the image of God, all forms of racial, ethnic, age, economic, or gender prejudice or supremacy are wrong. All humans come from the same place (God) and have the same being (God's image). We must treat all people with dignity, equality, compassion, and care.

Finally, reflecting the image of God is the primary way humans fulfill their purpose to glorify him. He created us for this purpose, to represent him to the rest of creation. We are not God, but we are mirrors of God and his glory.

TRAGIC FACT

If God created us in his image to reflect his glory, there is a problem: Our mirrors have been distorted by sin. Apart from his help, we cannot accurately and fully reflect God's glory. We will take this up in a few chapters. The solution is God's salvation through Jesus Christ.

Do Humans Have Parts?

We have seen that God is a perfect unity, with no parts to his being. In chapter 13, we noted that being created in the image of God means humans have some of the same characteristics as God. Is unity one of those characteristics? Or do humans have multiple parts? This is an issue of interest not only to theologians but also to psychologists. And your answer will affect both how you regard yourself as a person and how you treat other people.

Christians have rejected two extreme views. One of these, *reductive materialism*, asserts that humans are fundamentally material or physical. Aspects of our experience, such as our emotions, thoughts, even conscience, can ultimately be explained by brain chemistry or neuroscience. Naturalists hold this view, maintaining that there is no Creator God and no afterlife. When the body dies, the person dies.

At the other extreme is *radical dualism*, which declares that the human mind or soul (the person) and the body are separable. The body, which is just a temporary housing for the person, will eventually be unnecessary. This was the view of ancient

Greek philosophy: Physical death sets the individual free from a physical prison to exist immaterially for eternity.

Three Possible Views

Three views between these extremes are more consistent with the Bible and have been held through the centuries by Christians. The first of these is known as *monism* (also *physicalism* or *materialism*), which says that the person is a psychosomatic (from the Greek *psuchē*, meaning "soul," and *sōma*, meaning "body") unity. While similar to reductive materialism, monism does not hold that human functions are entirely explained by biological or chemical processes. Even so, it says that human existence is impossible apart from a physical body.

Monism interprets biblical terms like *body, soul,* and *spirit* as different references to the same thing—the person or self. Old Testament scholars suggest that this does seem to represent the Hebrew view of humans. However, New Testament texts indicate that it is possible for a person to exist temporarily without a physical body, in an "intermediate state" between physical death and physical resurrection. In 2 Corinthians 5:1–8, Paul refers to being "naked" (v. 3) and "unclothed" (v. 4) to describe our existence in heaven without a physical body. It is not ideal (we long "to be clothed," to have a physical body, vv. 2–4), but it is possible.

A second Christian view, the one that has been most widely held, is called *dualism* or *dichotomism* ("cut in two"). In this perspective, the person has two parts: the material and the immaterial. The material is the physical body; the immaterial includes the soul, spirit, and mind. Dualism does not, however, make a hard and fast distinction between these two aspects, which rely upon one another and function together.

Dualism fits with the intermediate state. After death, the material aspect is left behind in a grave. The immaterial aspect—the person—goes to heaven or hell to await resurrection.

A third Christian view, called *tripartism* (or *trichotomism*), says that the individual has three parts: body, soul (including intellect, emotions), and spirit (that which is able to relate to spiritual reality). The biblical argument for this view is verses that use all three terms (such as 1 Thessalonians 5:23) or that seem to distinguish between soul and spirit (such as Hebrews 4:12). Tripartism is not held by many biblical or theological scholars but is more popular among laypeople.

What We Can Ascertain About the Human Makeup

In response, first, we should acknowledge that biblical terms such as *body*, *soul*, *spirit*, *heart*, and *flesh* are broad and fluid. Like most words in any language, they do not mean the same thing every time they are used (meaning is determined by context). For example, sometimes *soul* and *spirit* refer to different things; sometimes they are used synonymously. So we should refrain from reaching invalid conclusions about what these terms always mean. We may want it to be, but it is not that simple.

Second, the Hebrew emphasis on the unity of the human individual is significant. God created us with a body, mind, volition, conscience, and emotions, and these all work together and depend on one another. And he wants to make us holy in all the various aspects of our united being. Paul says, "Let us purify ourselves from everything that contaminates body and spirit, perfecting holiness out of reverence for God" (2 Corinthians 7:1).

Third, in light of the biblical teaching regarding the intermediate state and verses like 2 Corinthians 7:1, it does seem valid to distinguish between material and immaterial. The best view seems to be a combination of monism and dichotomism. Millard Erickson refers to "conditional unity," the condition being the distinction between the material and the immaterial,[1] and Wayne Grudem speaks in terms of dichotomy "with overall unity."[2]

We can represent this as below. The material and the immaterial are different aspects of the individual, but rather than
a solid line separating them (implying a hard distinction), a
dashed line and arrows indicate close connection and interac-
tion between the two.

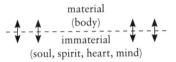

This makes sense out of how we experience life. Being injured
or sick does not only affect our bodies, it affects our attitudes and
emotions as well. When we don't feel well, we get grumpy. Similarly, when we are discouraged or depressed, we lose energy and
appetite; when we are happy, we feel full of energy and joy. This
seems to indicate how God has "knit together" (Psalm 139:13)
the aspects of our being. We may have different parts, but there
is a unity to—a close connection between—those parts as well.

Implications of How We Are Designed

One implication of this last observation is that as we offer
help to hurting people, we should probably not try to diagnose
their problem as being rooted in just one area and not others.
For example, depression may have emotional, psychological,
spiritual, and physical and/or biochemical aspects.

Another implication is that all these aspects are important and
valuable. Sometimes Christians (e.g., ascetics) have minimized
the importance of the body in favor of the soul/spirit. But Jesus
healed the sick and fed the starving, and called his followers to
do the same. In addition, there is the reality of the resurrection,
which will result in our having immortal physical bodies.

A final implication is implied by 2 Corinthians 7:1: Sin affects
every aspect of us, not just one. Some of the same Christians who

devalue the body have also thought that sin is simply a problem with our physical bodies. However, the Bible shows that we are tainted by sin in body *and* mind *and* will *and* conscience, and so on. Therefore, we should seek God's help in dealing with sin in every area of our lives.

INTERESTING FACT

Nephesh, the Hebrew word that often refers to the immaterial part of humans, is used several times of dead bodies! For example, "[The priest] must not enter a place where there is a dead body [*nephesh*]" (Leviticus 21:11), and "Throughout the period of their dedication to the Lord, the Nazirite must not go near a dead body [*nephesh*]" (Numbers 6:6). This term is *really* flexible.

What Is Sin?

This topic of theology can be unappealing because it is not enjoyable to think about and is so unflattering (to put it lightly) to us. Nevertheless, it is critical because it speaks to our perspectives on God, ourselves, the world around us, and the need for salvation based on God's grace alone.

Deviating From God

The most fundamental thing about sin is that it is whatever is contrary to God. He is perfect holiness; sin is anything that deviates in any way. Romans 3:23 says it best: "All have sinned and fall short of the glory of God."

God created us in his image to reflect his glory. However, due to sin, we can no longer perfectly or adequately do that. The divine mirrors that we were created to be have been distorted by sin.

Disobeying God

Another way of saying the same thing is that sin is disobeying God in any way. The commandments he has given to us are a reflection of his holy character. When we break them, we are acting contrary to who God is: "Everyone who sins breaks the law; in fact, sin is lawlessness" (1 John 3:4).

Another very fundamental truth about sin is that it is first and foremost something that happens inside us and only secondarily something we do or do not do on the outside. This is what Jesus was getting at when he said, "The things that come out of a person's mouth come from the heart, and these defile them. For out of the heart come evil thoughts—murder, adultery, sexual immorality, theft, false testimony, slander" (Matthew 15:18–19). The biblical concept of the heart includes our thoughts, attitudes, and motives. And these reflect who we truly *are*, from which comes what we *do*.

This is also what Jesus meant when he said that if you are angry with someone you are guilty of murder, because anger is the motive for murder (Matthew 5:21–22). If you lust after someone you are guilty of adultery, because lust is the motive for adultery (vv. 27–28).

This is why the first sin was probably committed, not when Eve and then Adam took the fruit from the forbidden tree and ate it (Genesis 3:6), but earlier when Eve seemed to question or doubt God's goodness (vv. 2–3). It was as though she were saying, "If God really loved me, he wouldn't restrict me; he would let me have whatever I want, and what I want is that fruit."

This becomes explicit a few chapters later, when the state of the world just before God's judgment through the flood is assessed in breathtaking terms: "The Lord saw how great the wickedness of the human race had become on the earth, and that every inclination of the thoughts of the human heart was only evil all the time" (6:5). Notice this is entirely about "inside stuff"—*inclination*, *thoughts*, and *heart*. Note also the universal terms: *every*, *only*, and *all the time*. No wonder God had to deal with it as he did.

So the biblical emphasis is not "we are sinners because we sin," but rather "we sin because we are sinners." It all begins with our fallen nature, what the Bible calls our "flesh" or, as the NIV renders the term, "sinful nature" (Romans 7:18; see also Galatians 5:16–24). My problem is not my sin; my problem is me! It is *fundamentally* who I am, not what I do. I have an inclination, a propensity, a "default setting" for sin.

This is why it is possible for God to assess "good" things as evil. Jesus strongly condemned the Pharisees for giving money to the poor, praying, and fasting—all good things in and of themselves. *Why* did Jesus condemn them? Because their *motives* were corrupt: They wanted the recognition and praise of people, not the glory of God (Matthew 6:1–2, 5, 16–17; see also Romans 1:21). Paul wrote, "Everything that does not come from faith is sin" (Romans 14:23). For our actions to be pleasing to God, to glorify him, we must do them in dependence upon him.

Further, that is why sinful acts are not only bad things we do (sins of commission) but also good things we do not do (sins of omission). Regarding the latter, James 4:17 says that if anyone "knows the good they ought to do and doesn't do it, it is sin for them."

Rebelling Against God

Sin likewise can be thought of as rebellion against and replacing God, in the place he alone deserves, by anything or anyone else. "[Sinners] exchanged the glory of the immortal God for images made to look like a mortal human being and birds and animals and reptiles" (Romans 1:23). To this list of "images" we could add reputation, fame, relationships, money, material goods, and much more. Read what Paul says in Romans 1:18–25 for an eye-opening description of sin's utter sinfulness.

What Sin Has Done

What has resulted from sin? Regarding ourselves, our experience is now dominated by death: "The wages of sin is death" (Romans 6:23). This is what God warned Adam about in Genesis 2:17 (compare Romans 5:12). *Death* means separation. So because of sin, our destiny is *physical* death—the separation of our immaterial being from our material bodies (Genesis 3:19; Hebrews 9:27). But it also includes something we experience every day: separation from God, or *spiritual* death. He is holy, and we are unholy: "You were dead in your transgressions and sins" (Ephesians 2:1; see also v. 5).

Spiritual death, however, is more than separation from God. It also includes "spiritual inability." Dead people can't do anything; spiritually dead people can't do anything spiritual. The term *total depravity* is also used for this terrible situation. "The mind governed by the flesh . . . does not submit to God's law, *nor can it do so*. Those who are in the realm of the flesh *cannot please God*" (Romans 8:7–8). Nothing within the sinner can impress or please God in any way, and the sinner can do nothing to solve the sin problem. *Only* God can do this.

Another result of sin is that we are slaves of our sinfulness (Romans 6:17–21). This means we are not free to do anything other than sin. Also, we live in deception (Jeremiah 17:9; Ephesians 4:17–18) because we think that our sinful state and actions are all right and even good, and that good and godly things are bad. This is because sinners hate God and are hostile toward him and what he says (Romans 8:7; James 4:4). These are just a few of sin's devastating results on all people.

What results from sin in terms of God? Not only are people separated from God in their unholiness but they also exist under his wrath (John 3:36; Romans 1:18; 2:5). This wrath will eventually result in God's judgment of sinners and their final, ultimate, eternal separation from him (Matthew 25:41; 2 Thessalonians 1:7–9; Revelation 20:11–15).

INTERESTING FACT

In anticipation of later chapters, we have just answered the question "Why does anyone need to be saved?" The answer is for all of the reasons mentioned above and more. Through Jesus Christ, God has addressed *all* these results of sin and solved *all* of sin's problems, and he has done it for free!

What Is Original Sin?

Within a hard-to-deal-with theological topic is a sub-topic that also is very hard to understand and come to grips with: *original sin*. The term basically refers to all people being born with a sin nature; each one of us is born a sinner. As noted in chapter 15, we are not sinners because we sin; rather, we sin because we are (born) sinners. The nature precedes the behavior; the acts flow from the condition.

It is called "original sin" because it traces back to the original sin of Adam. His sinful nature was passed on to his children and their children and therefore to all of humanity—as such, this is sometimes called "inherited sin." The Bible says, for example, "Surely I was sinful at birth, sinful from the time my mother conceived me" (Psalm 51:5; see also 58:3). In the New Testament we find:

All of us also lived among [the disobedient] at one time, grati-fying the cravings of our flesh and following its desires and thoughts. Like the rest, we were by nature [that is, from birth] deserving of wrath.

Ephesians 2:3

This means that at the point of conception, we all have the predisposition or inclination toward sin (see chapter 15). But not only do we have this propensity toward sin, God also rightly considers all of us guilty of sin. This is due to the imputation or transfer of Adam's guilt to the rest of humankind. Paul discusses this in Romans 5:12–19, beginning with

> Sin entered the world through one man [Adam], and death through sin, and in this way death came to all people, *because all sinned*—to be sure, sin was in the world before the law was given, but sin is not *charged against anyone's account* [transferred, imputed] where there is no law.

vv. 12–13

He concludes with

> Consequently, just as one trespass [Adam's sin] resulted in condemnation *for all people,* so also one righteous act [Jesus' sacrifice] resulted in justification and life for all people. For just as through the disobedience of the one man *the many were made sinners,* so also through the obedience of the one man the many will be made righteous.

vv. 18–19

Paul is saying that when Adam sinned, it's as if we all sinned; and just as Adam is guilty for that sin, so we all are guilty—for that sin. But how can that be? We are living thousands of years after the original sin, so how could God consider us guilty for that? Furthermore, how could this result in our being in a sinful

91

condition from the first moment of our lives? These are tough questions without easy answers.

Two Views on Original Sin

Some believe that Adam represented the rest of humanity in his life and specifically in his sin. This is called the *federal head* view of original sin. The U.S. has a federal government; for its legislative branch, we the people elect representatives to Congress. Their vote for or against a law is *their* vote, but it affects *us* as their constituents. In the same way, Adam is humanity's federal head. It was *his* act of sin, but as he is our representative, it affects us all.

Others believe that as God reckons things, when Adam sinned, all the rest of humanity was right there sinning along with him. So it is not only that his sin affects us because he represents us, but that his sin was our sin as well. This is called the *natural* or *realistic* view of original sin.

A fascinating passage that provides a biblical basis for this view is Hebrews 7:1–10, where the author reflects back on Abraham's encounter with Melchizedek (see Genesis 14). He concludes with "One might even say that Levi, who collects the tenth, paid the tenth through Abraham, because when Melchizedek met Abraham, Levi was still in the body of his ancestor" (vv. 9–10). Levi was three generations down the road from Abraham—many years from being born—yet it was just as if Levi himself had given this tithe, even though Abraham actually did. Why? Because "he was still in the body of his ancestor" just as we were "in the body of our ancestor, Adam," when he sinned.

However we understand it, it seems clear that from God's perspective, as a result of the first sin, every individual is born sinful and thus guilty.

A little history may help us here. Augustine was one of the earliest Christian thinkers to develop the doctrine of original sin. The view just described is essentially what he believed and taught. Thus his view was that all people are totally unable to help themselves and so are totally dependent upon the grace of God. This has come to be a tenet of Calvinism, but it is a hard position to embrace.

Another View (or Two or Three) on Original Sin

At the other end of the theological continuum, a British monk named Pelagius, a contemporary of Augustine, became convinced of just the opposite: Adam's sin did not affect the rest of us in any way. Rather, *Pelagianism* says we are sinners because *we* sin. Furthermore, Pelagius believed that because God commanded all people to be holy just as he is holy (Leviticus 11:44–45; 19:2; 20:7; 1 Peter 1:15–16), it must be possible. God wouldn't command us to do something we could not do. It is hypothetically possible, according to Pelagius, for a person to live a perfect and sin-free life.

Pelagius and Augustine battled it out through their writings, and Augustine "won" when the Council of Carthage condemned as heresy the teachings of Pelagius in AD 418. However, Augustine's view was still a bit too extreme for some, so a mediating position arose. *Semi-Pelagianism* denies that we are *totally* unable to do anything about our own sinful condition, but still we *are* in pretty bad shape and need a lot of help from God. If *we* initiate and reach out to God, he will respond. This cooperative view of salvation—the individual participates, God participates; together, salvation results—is the historic view of the Roman Catholic Church.

As the debate continued, yet another mediating view arose. Like semi-Pelagianism, *semi-Augustinianism* holds that we are not *totally* powerless; however, we are unable to reach out to God for help, so *God* must take the initiative. When he provides the help we need, then we can and must respond. This is basically the Arminian view.

As hard as it may be to understand and accept, the Bible does not paint an encouraging picture of our sinful condition and our ability to do anything about it. Sin has had devastating effects on all of us. As much as we might resist acknowledging this about ourselves, it is absolutely necessary that we do; it is the only way we can be saved. We must depend upon the grace of God *alone* through the work of Christ *alone*.

INTERESTING FACT

Many reject the idea that Adam's sinful act could so unavoidably affect the rest of us. It sounds unfair, and people don't like the idea of being guilty for what someone else has done. But according to Romans 5:12-19, the sacrificial act of one person, Jesus, also can thoroughly affect the rest of us—for righteousness! He died for sin, and through him we *all* can be right with God. To be consistent, if we reject universal human guilt coming from what Adam did, we must also reject the availability of righteousness being fully granted to us from what Christ did. We can't reject the first and accept the second; both are based on the same principle.

Why Should We Believe That Jesus Christ Is God?

One of the most remarkable foundations of the Christian faith is that Jesus Christ is eternal God. This is disputed by other religions (including the other monotheistic faiths, Judaism and Islam), by Mormons and Jehovah's Witnesses, and certainly by many skeptics. Without question, lacking this central pillar, Christianity fails and has nothing to offer anyone.

It is no surprise that from very early on, believers have contended for, fought for, and died for this teaching—the deity of Jesus Christ. In a nutshell, the doctrine is that Jesus Christ is fully God (not half God or one-third God) and eternally God (he did not become God at some point in time). Anything less has been considered heresy.

There are many lines of argument for the deity of Jesus. Plainly, the fact is crystal clear if one allows Scripture to say what it says. Here are a few of those contentions and a few examples.

Not only did Christ exist before he was conceived by Mary (this is what *preexistence* means), he has always been; he is eternal. John 1:1 says, "*In the beginning* was the Word [referring to Christ], and the Word was with God, and *the Word was God.*" This last phrase is also a straightforward statement of his deity. Jesus said, "Before Abraham was born, I am!" (John 8:58), both a declaration of eternality ("before Abraham was born") and of deity ("*I am*"). The Jews would have understood "I am" as a reference to the name of their God: Yahweh (see Exodus 3:14–15). That is why they immediately sought to kill him (John 8:59). The famous prophecy of Messiah's birthplace also says of him, "whose origins are from of old, from ancient times" (Micah 5:2).

Jesus Christ also has other divine attributes: omnipresence (demonstrated in his promise to be with all believers—e.g., Matthew 28:20), omnipotence (demonstrated through his miracles—e.g., Luke 8:23–25), and omniscience (demonstrated by his knowledge of human thoughts—e.g., Luke 6:8; 11:17). Only God has these three characteristics.

Another line of evidence is that Jesus Christ did what God does. For example, Jesus is Creator and sustainer of all things (John 1:3; Colossians 1:16–17; Hebrews 1:2–3). He gives life, specifically eternal life (John 5:21; 10:28; 11:25–26). A good example of Jesus' doing what only God can do is his forgiving the sins of a paralyzed man. The Jewish religious leaders responded, "Who can forgive sins but God alone?" *Exactly!* When Jesus healed the man, he said he did it because "I want you to know that the Son of Man has authority on earth to forgive sins" (see Mark 2:1–12).

In addition to being who God is and doing what God does, another evidence of his deity is that he made that claim himself: "I and the Father are one" (John 10:30; also 8:58, noted above). After his arrest, when the high priest demanded of Jesus, "Tell us if you are the Messiah, the Son of God" (Matthew 26:63), he replied, "You have said so. But I say to all of you: From now on you will see the Son of Man sitting at the right hand of the Mighty One and coming on the clouds of heaven" (v. 64). Here Jesus quotes from two messianic prophecies (Psalm 110:1; Daniel 7:13), and that those listening understood these as references to a divine being is indicated by their reaction: "He has spoken blasphemy! . . . He is worthy of death" (Matthew 26:65–66). This was the usual Jewish reaction to his claims of deity (e.g., John 8:59; 10:31).

Some claims that may seem obscure to us couldn't be missed by the Jews who heard Jesus, as evidenced by this same reaction. For example,

> "My Father is always at his work to this very day, and I too am working." For this reason they tried all the more to kill him; not only was he breaking the Sabbath, but he was even calling God his own Father, *making himself equal with God.*
>
> John 5:17–18

Another unavoidable argument for Christ's deity is that he accepted worship. He went so far as to say, "Whoever does not honor the Son does not honor the Father, who sent him" (v. 23). In other words, *if we don't worship him, we can't worship God.*

A little while after Jesus had given sight to the man born blind (John 9), he came back to this man, who had not yet *seen* him, and said, "Do you believe in the Son of Man?" When the man realized who this was, he said "'Lord, I believe,' and *he worshiped him*" (vv. 35–38). When Jesus appeared to his disciples after his resurrection (John 20), he said to Thomas, "'Stop doubting and believe.' Thomas said, 'My Lord and *my* God!'" (vv. 27–28).

What is so amazing about these examples is that these two loyal (strictly monotheistic) Jews did what they did. They believed in one God who has no physical form (thus the first and second commandments). Like others before them (e.g., see Daniel 3), they would rather have died than worship anyone but the one true God; the very thought was repugnant. But these men, like many others, worshiped Jesus because they had become completely convinced that this man *is* the one true God.

In historical context, what they did was absolutely revolutionary. And Jesus did not rebuke them. If thinking that he was God had revealed a terrible misunderstanding, Jesus could have taken the opportunity to say, "Hold on! Don't worship me! Worship only God" (as, for instance, Paul and Barnabas did, and as angels repeatedly did). Jesus accepted worship because he is God and is worthy of it.

One of the reasons this doctrine is so crucial is that if Jesus is not fully God, there is no salvation to be found in his death. The sacrifice that would be sufficient for the many sins of the many people had to be a sacrifice of *infinite* value. No human being could provide this kind of sacrifice; only God himself could. This is why the early Christians were so appalled at the deity of Jesus being denied. They knew his deity was absolutely vital for their salvation.

INTERESTING FACT

Two of the clearest New Testament texts regarding the deity of Jesus are Colossians 2:9: "In Christ *all the fullness of the Deity lives* in bodily form," and Hebrews 1:3: "The Son is the radiance of God's glory and *the exact representation of his being.*"

Why Should We Believe That Jesus Christ Is Human?

As we saw in chapter 17, orthodox Christianity has always proclaimed that Jesus Christ is fully and eternally God. It has also maintained that he became fully human as well. Small pockets of Christians have denied this, believing that he was truly God but not *truly* human; he only appeared to be a human, or only a part of him was human. This too was quickly considered heresy.

The true humanity of Jesus is just as important as his deity, for at least the following reason: As the sacrifice for the many sins of many humans had to be infinite in nature, so it had to be truly human. Only a human can die in the place of another human. That is why animal sacrifices could never accomplish this; they were only lessons about sin, not the payment for sin (Hebrews 10:3–4). God, who is of infinite value, *had* to become human in order to provide an adequate substitutionary sacrifice for sin (Hebrews 2:17).

Biblical Evidence for the Humanity of Jesus Christ

The New Testament epistle of 1 John is important in this regard. The apostle John was addressing the destructive influence of some who denied Christ's actual humanity. For example, he says,

> Every spirit that acknowledges that Jesus Christ has come *in the flesh* is from God, but every spirit that does not acknowledge Jesus is not from God. This is the spirit of the antichrist.
>
> 4:2–3

In light of this pressing issue, note how John began his epistle:

> That which was from the beginning, which we have heard, which we have seen with our eyes, which we have looked at and our hands have touched—this we proclaim concerning the Word of life.
>
> 1:1

"The Word" (*logos*) was John's way of referring to Jesus Christ (compare John 1:1). Obviously he did not waste any time getting started; he said, in essence, "I am an eyewitness! I have heard, seen, and touched Jesus. And I assure you he is not a phantom—he is utterly and fully human."

John was simply referring to his firsthand experience of what the New Testament records: Jesus was born, though not conceived, in a typical way (Luke 1–2). He had a human family tree (Matthew 1). He developed as a human (Luke 2:52). He had normal human needs (e.g., sleep, food, water). And he died physically (Matthew 27:50), as all humans do.

The New Testament refers to him as a "man"; Jesus presented himself as such (John 8:40). Paul, who referred to him as a man to Greek philosophers in Athens (Acts 17:31), also developed a key point involving the first man—Adam—and another man,

Jesus Christ, "the last Adam" (1 Corinthians 15:45; see Romans 5:12–21). This argument rests on Jesus' being as human as Adam, and his getting right what Adam got wrong for the benefit of all who would trust in him.

Paul says, "There is one *God* and one mediator between God and mankind, the *man* Christ Jesus" (1 Timothy 2:5). There it is in one verse—Jesus is both divine and human. As we saw in chapter 17, he made the same point elsewhere: "In Christ all the fullness of the Deity lives [his deity] in bodily form [his humanity]" (Colossians 2:9).

Another evidence of Jesus' true humanity is the term *Son of Man*. For example, Jesus said, "The Son of Man came to seek and to save the lost" (Luke 19:10). This term, rich in meaning, connotes even more than the fact that Jesus is human. The Old Testament background of many of the later uses of this term is Daniel 7:13–14:

> In my vision at night I looked, and there before me was *one like a son of man,* coming with the clouds of heaven. He approached the Ancient of Days [God] and was led into his presence. He was given authority, glory and sovereign power; all nations and peoples of every language *worshiped him.* His dominion is an everlasting dominion that will not pass away, and his kingdom is one that will never be destroyed.

This is a reference to the Messiah, as even some Jewish interpreters acknowledge and as early Christians came to understand. So not only is the Messiah human, he also comes from heaven (compare John 3:13; 6:62). This, combined with the fact that he will be worshiped by all people (Daniel 7:14), implies his deity. "Son of Man" means not only that the Messiah is fully human but also that he is God at the same time.

What Christ's Humanity Means for Us

In addition to qualifying him to die in our place for our sin, there are other benefits from the humanity of Jesus. One of the most amazing is that he is sympathetic to what it means to be human, and more specifically, to know human *weakness*.

> Since we have a great high priest who has ascended into heaven, Jesus the Son of God, let us hold firmly to the faith we profess. For we do not have a high priest who is unable to empathize with our weaknesses, but we have one who has been tempted in every way, just as we are—yet he did not sin.
>
> Hebrews 4:14–15

That is why, as the following verse says, we can "approach God's throne of grace with confidence, so that we may receive mercy and find grace to help us in our time of need" (v. 16). Jesus has experienced humanity, so he can relate to us and, through his Father, provide what we need. This is truly a precious promise.

Another benefit for us is that being a human, Jesus shows what God intended us to be as his image-bearers. Jesus' humanity is a perfect humanity, untouched by sin. So in him, we see what we as Christians will be when all our sin and fallenness has been removed once and for all, that is, the kind of humanity we will experience for all eternity.

These days, not many people deny the humanity of Jesus. As a matter of fact, most people would prefer to think he was *only* human. That is because the humanity of Jesus is not threatening to anyone. On the other hand, his deity seems threatening, because if Jesus is truly God, we must *submit* to him, *honor* him, and *obey* him, and this is not what sinful people want to do. Nevertheless, both the full humanity *and* deity of Jesus are inseparable from Christianity and our hope of salvation through him.

INTERESTING FACT

All occurrences of the term *Son of Man* (more than eighty) are in the Gospels, except one, and all are said by Jesus except one. This was his *favorite* way of referring to himself; he demonstrated that he gladly and frequently identified himself with lowly humans, the ones he created and came to save.

How Can Jesus Be
Both God and Man?

In the last two chapters we considered Jesus Christ as God and human and examined why both are so vital. Now we ask, "How can this be? How can both of these be true of one individual at the same time?" Because this is so mysterious, so hard to understand, many have denied it and concluded that either Jesus was God or he was human, but not both.

The Joining of Two Natures in One Person

The taking on of humanity is called the incarnation. The eternal Son of God, the second person of the Trinity, took humanity upon himself, in addition to his deity, and became, *forever,* fully God and fully human. The means of the incarnation was the virgin birth of Jesus. Mary became pregnant through the power of the Holy Spirit, and she gave birth both to someone who had always been—the Son of God—and to a facet of him that was entirely new—the God-man, Jesus. This was foretold in the Old Testament in Isaiah 7:14, "The virgin will conceive and give birth to a son." Matthew quoted this verse and understood the fulfillment to be in Jesus (Matthew 1:22–23). John wrote, "The Word [Christ] became flesh and made his dwelling among us" (John 1:14).

The incarnation is key to our faith for a number of reasons. One is that as a result, we can understand God much better. For example, John 1:18 says, "No one has ever seen God [he is spirit and therefore invisible], but the one and only Son [a clear reference to Jesus, see v. 14], who is himself God and is in closest relationship with the Father, has made him known [explained him]." When we look at Jesus in the Gospels, we are looking at God. This is a tremendous advantage in seeking to comprehend who God is.

Another reason for the incarnation's importance is that it tells us of God's desire to be near to and involved in his creation (*immanence*), so much so that he became a part of his creation when the Son took a created thing—a human nature—upon himself *forever*. As we have already seen, both natures, divine and human, were necessary in order to provide the needed and sufficient sacrifice for sin. All this speaks of God's marvelous love for those whom he created in his image.

The theological term for the result of the incarnation is *hypostatic union*, which refers to the union of two natures in one person (the Greek word is *hupostasis*). This one person is *fully* God and *fully* human (not half God and half human, or part God and part human).

One key text that speaks of this union is Philippians 2:1–8. Here Paul encourages persecuted Christians to be in unity, and he gives them Jesus as the great model to follow: "Have the same mindset as Christ Jesus" (v. 5). He goes on to describe Jesus, using very precise terms:

Who, being in very nature God [a clear reference to his
    deity],
did not consider equality with God something to be
    used to his own advantage;
rather, he made himself nothing
by taking the very nature of a servant [God, serving us!
    (Matthew 20:28)],
being made in human likeness [*likeness* refers to simi-
    larities and differences: Jesus was truly human, but
    he was also God].
And being found in appearance as a man [*appearance*
    refers to outward form, meaning that Jesus looked
    like any other human because he had a body like any
    other human],
he humbled himself
by becoming obedient to death—
    even death on a cross!

vv. 6–8

Back, then, to our main question: *How* can this union be? It is a mystery, and neither I nor any other person fully understands it, much less can explain it. Ultimately we accept it because it is what Scripture teaches. But there are some other truths that will help.

A Bit More Clarification

First, the incarnation does not mean that Christ gave up any of his divine attributes. Some have tried to argue (from Philippians 2:7) that this *is* what he did. Paul says he "made himself nothing" [literally, "emptied himself"]. However, if he gave up divine attributes, he gave up his deity altogether. A divine nature is the sum of all divine attributes, and God can't cease to be God any more than we can cease to be human (we are who we are by nature). Rather, "made himself nothing" is best understood as a reference to Christ's willingness to humble himself, by leaving the glories of heaven and his Father's immediate presence, and identifying himself with his sinful and lowly creatures, humans (v. 8), living here among us and dying for us.

Second, even though Jesus did not give up any divine attributes, after the incarnation he did limit the exercise of some of them. "Made himself nothing" may imply this. For example, there are references to his doing things in the Holy Spirit's power (Matthew 12:28; Luke 4:14; Acts 10:38). Why? As God, he had the same unlimited power as God's Spirit. So this was likely a part of his identifying with us; humans are not omnipotent and need to rely upon God's power.

Similarly, Jesus himself said he could do nothing apart from his Father (John 5:19, 30). Jesus was not saying he was no longer omnipotent. Rather, it speaks of his submission to his Father's will (John 6:38). There were also some things that, as a human, Jesus did not know, even though, as God, he is omniscient (Mark 13:32). So in his deity, Jesus could do anything and knew everything; in his humanity, he experienced weakness and dependence and did not know all things. *Truly* mysterious!

AMAZING FACT

Twice above, I emphasized the word *forever* in reference to Jesus' becoming human. Some people think the Son of God's dual nature lasted thirty years or so, but when Jesus left earth and returned to his Father, he left his humanity behind. That is not the case—the incarnation was never reversed! This demonstrates the extent of Christ's love for and willingness to identify with humans. Accepting a human nature, with all of its weaknesses and limitations, was an astonishing act of humiliation on the part of infinite, omnipotent God. It would have been amazing for him to do it for a mere few decades—how *amazingly* amazing that he was willing to do it forever.

What Has Jesus Christ Done?

In previous chapters we have considered the work of God in creation and providence. Now we answer the question "What is the work of God's Son, more specifically?"

Before the Incarnation

Since the Son of God is eternal, we begin with noting his work before the incarnation, before Christ took upon himself a human nature. With the Father and the Spirit, Christ was involved in creation (John 1:3; Colossians 1:16–17; Hebrews 1:2). More on this in chapter 22, where we consider his lordship.

Another important aspect of Christ's Old Testament work was delivering God's messages. The "angel [messenger] of the LORD [*Yahweh*]" normally is understood to be Christ himself, and the technical term for these occurrences is *theophany* (appearance of God). These are pre-incarnation manifestations of the Son of God in human form—Christ took upon himself human appearance to accomplish something specific before taking upon himself a permanent human nature (in the incarnation).

This "angel" is no ordinary angel. For example, when Hagar fled into the desert after conceiving Abram's son, the angel of the LORD told her to name her son Ishmael and to return to the household of Abram (Genesis 16:7–14). Verse 13 says, "She gave this name to the LORD who spoke to her: 'You are the God who sees me,' for she said, 'I have now seen the One who sees me.'" Hagar understood this individual to be God himself. Similarly, in Judges 6:11–22, the angel of the LORD came to Gideon to declare that God was with him (v. 11); in verse 14, he is simply referred to as "the LORD" (*Yahweh*).

After the Incarnation

The Son's primary work, however, was after the incarnation, specifically to die in the place of sinful humanity. This is so significant that we will devote an entire chapter to it (chapter 26) when we address the doctrine of salvation.

A common way of thinking about Jesus' post-incarnation work is in terms of three biblical offices. All human prophets, priests, and kings among God's people were anticipations or symbols of the ultimate prophet-priest-king: Jesus Christ. The great prophet Moses anticipated a greater prophet (Deuteronomy 18:15). Jesus did do what prophets do: deliver God's message to God's people (Matthew 21:11; Luke 13:33; John 17:8). Not only did he deliver the message, he *is* the message; he is the Word of God (John 1:1).

Jesus is also our high priest, like Aaron and his sons initially were. He did what priests do: represent God's people in God's presence by bringing their sacrifices and offerings. Not only did he bring the sacrifice to God, he *is* the sacrifice (Hebrews 7:27; 10:10), and unlike Aaron and his sons, Jesus' priesthood is in the order of Melchizedek (Genesis 14:18–20; Hebrews 5:6–10;

6:20–7:17). Jesus was not a descendant of Aaron and so was not qualified for that priesthood. But the priesthood of Melchizedek united two offices—priest and king (Genesis 14:18; Zechariah 6:13)—which brings us to the third.

As a descendant of David, Jesus was qualified to be king on David's throne (Luke 1:32–33). Isaiah prophesied that the Messiah would be a king (Isaiah 9:7). Jesus acknowledged before Pilate that he was indeed king of the Jews (Matthew 27:11), as the crowds at his triumphal entry recognized (John 12:13). When Jesus returns, he will reign on earth (Revelation 17:14; 19:16) in fulfillment of the Davidic Covenant, which promised David an eternal throne (2 Samuel 7:16).

Here is another question often considered in connection with Christ's earthly life and work: Even though Jesus did not sin (Hebrews 4:15; 1 John 3:5), *could* he have sinned (hypothetically)? Some believe he could have (the peccability of Christ); others believe it was impossible for him to have sinned (the impeccability of Christ). There are strong arguments on both sides.

Those who believe he could have sinned argue that a part of being truly human is the freedom to rebel against God. Jesus, being truly human, should also have this freedom. Another argument for Christ's peccability is from Hebrews 4:15, which says he "is [able] to empathize with our weaknesses" because he "has been tempted in every way, just as we are." How could he sympathize with our weaknesses and our experience of temptation if it was impossible for him to ever yield to it? That would be a tremendous advantage we do not have. So for him to be truly empathetic with our struggle, it seems there must have been at least the possibility of his yielding to temptation.

Those who argue for Christ's impeccability point out that he is fully God. God is holy and cannot sin—his divine nature makes sin impossible for him. In regard to the contention (above) from Hebrews 4:15, it is suggested that feeling the force of temptation and yielding to temptation are different. Jesus could have felt the temptation to sin even if he could not possibly have yielded to it. And if this is true, then he felt the force of temptation to a degree that no other human would feel it, for the very reason that he never gave in to it.

Maybe the best conclusion is that in his human nature alone, Jesus was able to sin like any other human, but when his humanity was united to his deity—as the one person of the God-man—he was not able to sin. But it also seems likely that he did not rely on this impeccability when he dealt with temptation. Rather, he relied upon the Holy Spirit's power. And in this way, he truly is our model in dealing with temptation. We do not have divine natures to keep us from sin (like he did), but we do have the divine resident within us through the Holy Spirit, whose limitless power is available to help us in our fight against sin (Galatians 5:16–25). This is what Jesus modeled for us.

After the Ascension

Next, we need to consider Christ's work in the present. Succinctly stated, as the head of his church (Ephesians 1:22–23; Colossians 1:18)—all those who have believed in him as Savior— he is lovingly working to bring it to individual and corporate maturity. He is doing all that is necessary to make Christians a worthy bride for himself forever (Ephesians 5:25–29). As noted above, a part of that work is to act as our high priest in the presence of his Father (Hebrews 4:14–16). In that role, he is also interceding for us (Romans 8:34: Hebrews 7:25) and defending us as our advocate (1 John 2:1).

With regard to Christ's work in the future, we have seen that he will return to earth, defeat his enemies, establish his kingdom, rule and reign over that kingdom, and judge all people to determine their eternal destiny (more on this in the closing chapters).

INTERESTING FACT

More than half of the four Gospels are comprised of the words of Jesus (the red letters, in some versions). Those writers truly grasped the importance of Christ's teaching in terms of his work on earth.

Is the Resurrection of Jesus Really That Important?

The bodily, historical resurrection of Jesus is surely the most momentous event in all of history. I say "bodily" because many have said they believe in the resurrection of Jesus, but it is a spiritual resurrection, not a bodily one. The thinking is that Jesus becomes spiritually "alive" within a person. I say "historical" because many others have denied that Jesus was resurrected as a historical event. The naturalistic mindset certainly resists believing such a magnificent miracle.

Is this really all that important? Isn't it really the *death* of Jesus that is of ultimate significance for Christianity? Wouldn't it be easier for many more people to believe if the resurrection were not a central part of what Christians believe—or at least if it were easier to make sense of it?

Why the Resurrection Is Centrally Imperative

In truth, Christ's resurrection is absolutely vital to Christianity and our salvation, and as such, the fact appears in the earliest creeds of the faith, two of them being the Apostles' Creed and the Nicene Creed. Paul wrote of it in 1 Corinthians 15, his great chapter on resurrection. He included it in his succinct statement of the gospel itself in verses 1–8 (note especially verse 4). The problem he was addressing was that some were saying, "There is no resurrection of the dead" (v. 12), that is, the resurrection is not an important part of the gospel or of faith in Christ. Paul is unambiguous in his response:

> If there is no resurrection of the dead, then not even Christ has been raised. And if Christ has not been raised, our preaching is useless *and so is your faith. . . . [In that case] you are still in your sins.*
>
> vv. 13–14, 17

If Jesus were not brought back from the dead after his sacrifice, *there would be no salvation.* We would have nothing to believe, nothing to put our faith in.

So why is Jesus' resurrection so vital? First, his resurrection was essentially the Father's "stamp of approval" on Jesus' substitutionary sacrifice. The Father accepted his work, and the basis for the plan of salvation was successfully laid. In his great Pentecost sermon, the apostle Peter said, "God has raised this Jesus to life, and we are all witnesses of it. [He is] exalted to the right hand of God . . . " (Acts 2:32–33; see also Philippians 2:8–9). The Father exalted his Son for successfully accomplishing what he had been sent to do: to die in our place and pay for our sins. This is why Paul can say, "[Jesus] was delivered over to death for our sins and was *raised to life for our justification*" (Romans 4:25).

Second, his resurrection demonstrates that Christ's death defeated death:

> When the perishable has been clothed with the imperishable, and the mortal with immortality [that is, after resurrection],

then the saying that is written will come true: "Death has been swallowed up in victory."

"Where, O death, is your victory?
Where, O death, is your sting?"

The sting of death is sin, and the power of sin is the law. But thanks be to God! He gives us the victory through our Lord Jesus Christ.

1 Corinthians 15:54–57

A Savior who was conquered by death could not himself conquer death. But Jesus was not conquered by death—just the opposite is true. His resurrection is evidence of this great victory (2 Timothy 1:10; Hebrews 2:14–15).

Third, his resurrection provides spiritual life for believers in him, that is, it results in their regeneration—being born again. "In [God's] great mercy he has given us new birth into a living hope through the resurrection of Jesus Christ from the dead" (1 Peter 1:3). Related to this is that Christians have *already* experienced *spiritual* resurrection, even as we await physical resurrection (Ephesians 2:5–6).

And it gets even better, because all this means believers have access to the same divine power that brought Jesus back from the dead (Ephesians 1:18–20; Philippians 3:10). Specifically, this power helps us defeat sin. Paul says we have been united with Christ in both his death and resurrection, and for this reason he can say,

Count yourselves dead to sin but *alive to God in Christ Jesus.* Therefore do not let sin reign in your mortal body so that you obey its evil desires. Do not offer any part of yourself to sin as an instrument of wickedness, but rather offer yourselves to God *as those who have been brought from death to life;* and offer every part of yourself to him as an instrument of righteousness.

Romans 6:11–13 (See vv. 3–14.)

Fourth, his resurrection is the *firstfruits* of resurrection (1 Corinthians 15:20, 23). This Old Testament term refers to the very first part of the harvest, given in thanks to God for providing it. But the firstfruits also guarantee latter fruits, that is, there is more of the harvest to come. So as firstfruits, Jesus' resurrection guarantees the resurrection of believers in him.

Colossians 1:18 and Revelation 1:5 make the same point by referring to Jesus as the *firstborn* from the dead. Again, believers have experienced spiritual resurrection and await physical resurrection, which is guaranteed by Jesus' resurrection. This is a part of our hope in him and the completion of our eternal humanity (1 Corinthians 6:14; 2 Corinthians 4:14; remember, to be human is to have a physical body).

Finally, Jesus' resurrection should encourage Christians to be faithful in obeying and working for the Lord. This is Paul's concluding statement at the end of 1 Corinthians 15:

> Therefore, my dear brothers and sisters, stand firm. Let nothing move you. Always give yourselves fully to the work of the Lord, because you know that your labor in the Lord is not in vain.

> v. 58

Jesus' resurrection, the basis for *our* hope of resurrection, means that, when all is said and done, all the hard work of being faithful to Christ in this life will be more than worth it.

The Resurrection Is a Historical Event

The resurrection of Jesus is inseparable from salvation and must be believed as part of the gospel itself. And no one is foolish to embrace faith in his bodily, historical resurrection. The solid evidence for it includes the post-resurrection appearances of Jesus to many people, including the women at the tomb (Matthew 28:1–10), the apostles (Luke 24:36–49), and hundreds of others (1 Corinthians 15:6). Those who saw him were convinced Jesus was very much alive. And many of them, including the apostles, died for their faith in the resurrected Jesus Christ; people do not give their lives for what they know to be a lie.

INTERESTING FACT

Frank Morison was a British journalist who set out to prove that Christ's resurrection never happened. As he investigated whether there was any legally acceptable evidence for it, he became so convinced by the sufficient and compelling support he found that he wrote *Who Moved the Stone: A Skeptic Looks at the Death and Resurrection of Jesus* (Zondervan, 1987). Its first chapter—"The Book That Refused to Be Written"—reflects his conversion.

What Does It Mean to Say That Jesus Is Lord?

Jesus is Lord" is a well-known declaration among Christians. We talk often about the lordship of Christ. What does this really mean? Do we understand what we are saying? I wonder if the answer is that we understand *part* of this truth—Jesus is God; Jesus is our Savior—but usually not its full extent. Biblically, it is a breathtaking concept, and we *must* come to grips with it. (In my opinion, this could be one of this book's most important chapters.)

Very briefly, the lordship of Jesus Christ ought to mean that everything in this universe is about Jesus. *Everything. EVERY-THING.* This may sound like an overstatement, but it is thoroughly scriptural. It summarizes everything the Bible has to say about him—and that is a lot!

A Key Passage on Christ's Lordship

Here is some of what Paul said in his letter to the Colossians. Note the emphasized words:

The Son is the image of the invisible God, the firstborn over *all* creation. For in him *all* things were created: things in heaven and on earth, visible and invisible, whether thrones or powers or rulers or authorities; *all* things were created through him and for him. He is before *all* things, and in him *all* things hold together. And he is the head of the body, the church; he is the beginning and the firstborn from among the dead, so that in *everything* he might have the supremacy. For God was pleased to have *all* his fullness dwell in him, and through him to reconcile to himself *all* things, whether things on earth or things in heaven, by making peace through his blood, shed on the cross.

1:15–20

The universal terms Paul uses here—*all* and *everything*—are repeated and significant, and he does not use them lightly. Consider just a few of the wonderful realities Paul conveys.

Two statements are about the deity of Jesus: He "is the image of the invisible God" (v. 15) and "God was pleased to have all his fullness dwell in him" (v. 19). So Jesus is Lord because he is God; *all* that is true of God is true of Jesus Christ.

In the second phrase of verse 15, the Greek word translated *firstborn* means "prior to" (in terms of time) and "priority over" (in terms of status). Here, primarily, Paul probably had "priority over" in mind: Christ is superior over all creation. Verse 16 explains why: "In him all things were created." As we have seen, that is one of the indications of his deity—he does what God does, in this case, create. Christ is Lord because he is the creator of *all* things.

Not only do all things find their source in Christ, but all things find their purpose in him, as Paul says at the end of verse 16: "All things were created in him *and for him.*" He is the beginning of all and the end of all, the target toward which creation is moving. Furthermore, "in him all things hold together" (v. 17). This means he is sustainer of all things: He got everything going, and he keeps everything going. He is the glue *and* the goal of creation; Christ holds together everything he has made so that it will fulfill its intended purpose: *himself.* Paul summed this up elsewhere: "From him and through him and for him are all things" (Romans 11:36).

So in verses 15–17, Paul has focused on Christ's nature as eternal God and on his work of creation. In verse 18, he begins speaking of Christ's nature after adding humanity to his eternal deity (the incarnation) and his work of *re-creation.* The problem is, our sin has corrupted what he created and cannot now accomplish what he intended. So now it is necessary to correct through re-creation or reconciliation what we have corrupted. This too he does.

Paul now says Christ "is the head [Lord] of the body, the church; he is the beginning and the firstborn [again, has priority over] from among the dead" [those who will be resurrected to eternal life]. All of this is true because of his work as Savior. In verse 20, Paul says God was pleased "through [Christ] to reconcile to himself all things, whether things on earth or things in heaven, by making peace through his blood, shed on the cross." But notice the purpose statement at the end of verse 18: "so that in everything he might have the supremacy." In other words, "so that in *everything* Christ might be *Lord.*"

It's All About Jesus

As Dr. Duane Litfin, a former professor of mine, has put it, we live in a "Son-centered" universe.[1] It *is* all about Jesus Christ. Does this idea slight the Trinity? Absolutely not, and part of the reason is clear in this very text: "God [the Father] was pleased to have all his fullness dwell in him [the Son]" (v. 19). This is what the Father intended all along; it was his plan, his will. Son-centeredness glorifies the Father, a point Paul also makes elsewhere:

At the name of Jesus every knee should bow
in heaven and on earth and under the earth,
and every tongue acknowledge that Jesus Christ is Lord,
to the glory of God the Father.

Philippians 2:10–11

What about the Spirit? Jesus himself said, "[The Spirit] will *glorify me* because it is from me that he will receive what he will make known to you" (John 16:14). The Spirit himself is Christ-centered—willingly, gladly. Christ-centeredness glorifies the Trinity! Dr. Litfin puts it like this: "It was the Father's design that not just the Christian faith, but the entire cosmos he created, be profoundly Son-centered."[2] We live in a Christ-centered universe by the Father's design and the Spirit's disclosure. *That* is why Christ is Lord of *all*.

Everything in this universe is from Jesus Christ, about Jesus Christ, and for Jesus Christ. This is what Christians *should* mean when they say Jesus is Lord. The implications of this are *staggering*! Think them through.

INTERESTING FACT

Colossians 1:15 yields yet another brilliant truth about Jesus Christ: He is "the image of the invisible God." God, the most wonderful being in the universe, is "invisible" or inaccessible to us. However, because he wants to be known, he has graciously given us an "image" (likeness, representation) of himself. The Greek term is *eikōn,* from which we get the English word *icon.* As clicking on an icon gives us access to all the helpful things digitally "hidden" on a computer's hard drive, so Jesus Christ gives us access to God and to all the wealth of help and knowledge to be found in him.

Is the Holy Spirit a Person or Thing?

The Holy Spirit has sometimes been called the "forgotten" member of the Trinity. We automatically think of the Father when we think of God, and Jesus Christ is our Savior and Lord. All too often, though, little attention is given to the Spirit.

There is a sad reality to this assessment, because first, the Spirit is God and thus deserves our utmost focus, and second, he is a precious gift to believers, providing vital resources for us to live the *spirit*ual life. Not only is it he who gives us spiritual life (John 3:5–8), it is also he who nurtures us spiritually, giving us the ability to mature in godliness (Romans 8:1–16; Galatians 5:16–25). We dare not neglect him, for to do so is to miss out on so much that God intends for us. As we will see in the next three chapters, the Spirit has been sent to work for our benefit in amazing ways.

Person and *Power*

As we get to know the Spirit better, we must first acknowledge him as a person. Throughout church history, several Christian groups have denied this fact, e.g., Socinians (a thoroughly heretical group that denied most of the faith's foundational truths), and Unitarians (who deny God's Trinitarian nature). These have understood the Spirit as a way of referring to the power of God—an impersonal thing rather than a personal being.

It is true that the Spirit is closely associated with God's power. When Gabriel told Mary she was going to bear a baby—Messiah—even though she was a virgin, he explained, "The Holy Spirit will come on you, and the power of the Most High will overshadow you" (Luke 1:35). Paul wrote, "My message and my preaching were not in persuasive words of wisdom, but in demonstration of the Spirit and of power" (1 Corinthians 2:4 NASB; see also Micah 3:8). The Spirit was responsible for empowering Jesus during his life on earth (Luke 4:14; see also Acts 10:38).

However, this does not mean that "the Holy Spirit equals God's power." Rather, and significantly, the Holy Spirit himself is a channel of God's power. It is precisely this power that is made available to weak people like us so that we can do what God calls us to do and be what God calls us to be (Acts 1:8; Romans 8:26; 15:13; Ephesians 3:16).

How the Spirit Is Revealed As a Person

A number of lines of biblical evidence show that the Spirit is a person.

First, by definition a person is a being with intelligence, emotion, and will. The Spirit has all three: Paul refers to the "mind of the Spirit" (Romans 8:27, *intelligence*); he reminds us that the Spirit can be grieved (Ephesians 4:30, *emotion*); and he says that the Spirit distributes spiritual gifts "just as he determines" (1 Corinthians 12:11, *will*).

Second, the Spirit performs the kinds of actions a person performs. For example, as Paul was spreading the gospel of Jesus Christ, the Spirit was directing him as to where he should and should not go (Acts 16:6–10). The Spirit intercedes or prays for Christians (Romans 8:26). He does miraculous works (Acts 8:39).

Third, the grammar of John 16:13–14 is worth noting. Normally, a pronoun matches in gender (masculine, feminine, or neuter) the noun it replaces. The Greek noun translated "spirit" is *pneuma* (which is neuter). Yet John (recording Jesus' words) uses the masculine pronoun (he) twice:

> When *he,* the Spirit of truth, comes, he will guide you into all the truth. He will not speak on his own; he will speak only what he hears, and he will tell you what is yet to come. *He* will glorify me because it is from me that he will receive what he will make known to you. (The non-italicized masculine pronouns are implied in the verbs.)

Normal usage of the language did not include a personal identification for *spirit,* but John recorded what technically was grammatically incorrect in order to be theologically correct in clarifying that the Spirit is a person, not a thing.

This is important practically because we cannot have a *personal* relationship with a thing, only with another person. Being a Christian means we are in a personal relationship with the triune God—three persons in one divine essence. As is true of any relationship that matters to us, we should want to nurture our relationship with God the Father and with God the Son *and* with God the Spirit.

For instance, even though there are no biblical examples, I believe it is theologically correct and spiritually vital that we talk to the Spirit (pray)—ask him for his help and ask him to do what God has promised he will do for us *through his Spirit.*

In the next two chapters, we also will see that we are to live by, be led by, and follow the Spirit (Galatians 5:16–25). All of this implies a healthy and growing personal relationship with the Holy Spirit.

How the Spirit Is Revealed As God

As we acknowledge the Spirit's personhood, we also must acknowledge his deity—he is fully God, equal in every way with the Father and the Son.

For one thing, he has the attributes that make God *God*. For example, Psalm 139:7 seems to assume his omnipresence: "Where can I go from your Spirit? Where can I flee from your presence?" As we have seen, he is the channel of God's power, implying his omnipotence. His full title—*Holy* Spirit—assumes the divine attribute of holiness.

Further, the Spirit does what God does. He was involved in creation (Genesis 1:2; Psalm 104:30; this also implies omnipotence). He inspired Scripture (2 Samuel 23:2; 2 Peter 1:21). He gives life (John 6:64).

Also, the Spirit is mentioned equally with the Father and Son in, for instance, the Great Commission: "Go and make disciples of all nations, baptizing them in the name of the Father and of the Son and of the Holy Spirit" (Matthew 28:19; see also 2 Corinthians 13:14; 1 Peter 1:2).

Therefore, not only do we need to nurture our relationship with the Holy Spirit because he is a person, we also need to worship and adore him because he is God.

INTERESTING FACT

Many Christians refer to the Holy Spirit with the pronoun *it,* as in, "The Holy Spirit came on the day of Pentecost—*it* gave the Christians great power to witness for Jesus." Although probably or usually not intentional, this is essentially a denial of his personhood. Even worse, this could be taken as demeaning of the Spirit, like with the frustrated child who, agitated with her younger brother, demands of her mom, "Tell *IT* to leave me alone!" Let's discipline ourselves to refer to the Spirit with personal pronouns: *he, him, his.*

How Does the Holy Spirit Help Christians?

Because the Holy Spirit is fully God, he is omnipresent and has always been active in the world. However, Pentecost marks an expanded work of the Spirit for the benefit of those who have believed in Christ as Savior.

Jesus anticipated this when he told his followers to return to Jerusalem after his ascension and wait for the coming of the promised Spirit, who would enable them to be his witnesses (Acts 1:4–8). That promise was fulfilled on the day of Pentecost when the Spirit "filled" the believers (2:1–4). Peter links that occasion with a prophecy in Joel 2:28–32 of the pouring out of the Spirit (Acts 2:14–21). This expanded ministry is vitally important, so let us look at some of the Holy Spirit's ministries discussed in the New Testament.

Baptism of the Spirit

Both John the Baptist (Matthew 3:11; John 1:33) and Jesus (Acts 1:5) predicted the *baptism of the Spirit*. Peter understood that this was first fulfilled on the day of Pentecost (Acts 11:15–16). The one reference in the epistles is 1 Corinthians 12:13: "We were all baptized by one Spirit so as to form one body—whether Jews or Gentiles, slave or free—and we were all given the one Spirit to drink." Paul implies that this is true of *all* Christians, since he said, "we were *all* baptized" and used the past-tense verb. So this is not something Christians should seek, for it is already true of all. Furthermore, the result is that the believer is identified with (the meaning of *baptize*) the body of Christ, that is, all other believers corporately.

Indwelling, Sealing, Filling

All Christians also benefit from the *indwelling of the Spirit*. He is given as a gift of God (Acts 1:4; Romans 5:5) to actually live within the believer. And this becomes a defining characteristic of those who belong to Christ:

> You . . . are not in the realm of the flesh but are in the realm of the Spirit, if indeed the Spirit of God lives in you. And if anyone does not have the Spirit of Christ, they do not belong to Christ.
>
> Romans 8:9

This is also significant because Christians become the very temple of God (1 Corinthians 3:16; 6:19). What a reality—the God of the universe dwells within us through his Spirit!

The *sealing of the Spirit* is another benefit to believers (2 Corinthians 1:22; Ephesians 1:13–14; 4:30). A seal is a mark of ownership and authority. So the Holy Spirit living within the Christian is God's mark of ownership and authority over that individual.

More than that, a seal is a mark of security. You don't mess with a seal. The point is that one should not mess with those upon whom God has placed his seal; those who do will suffer the consequences.

One more associated idea is that this is "a deposit, guaranteeing what is to come" (2 Corinthians 1:22; see also Ephesians 1:14). Think of this as a "down payment," a partial disbursement giving assurance that the rest will eventually come. As we will see later, God has promised us wonderful things. *Some* of those are a part of the believer's present experience, but the rest will be experienced in the future—our inheritance in Christ. The sealing of the Spirit is God's absolute guarantee that *all* he has promised us *will* ultimately be ours. One practical application of this ministry of the Spirit is to give us an assurance of our salvation. No one can break God's seal or frustrate him from fulfilling his promises to his own.

There are many New Testament references to the *filling of the Spirit* (e.g., Luke 1:15, 41, 67; Act 2:4; 4:8, 31; 6:3, 5). We are commanded to be filled with him: "Do not get drunk on wine, which leads to debauchery. Instead, be filled with the Spirit" (Ephesians 5:18).

Notably, it's instructive to compare two other references that link drinking or drunkenness with this idea (Luke 1:15; Acts 2:4 and 13). Both have to do with an influence upon a person resulting in a significant character change. A drunken person is easily identified by acting in an uncharacteristic way; similarly, the Spirit transforms the Christian with the character of Jesus Christ.

Also, both influences are related to choices made. A person chooses to consume alcohol excessively to become drunk. In the same way, Paul putting this in the form of a command implies that being filled with the Spirit is a choice we make to yield ourselves to his positive influence.

Finally, both influences can "wear off." The drunken person eventually sobers up, unless he takes in more alcohol. And since

Christians are still sinful, we tend to turn away from the Spirit's positive influence and seek control of our own lives. That is why, based on the grammar of this command, we really are to "*keep on being* filled by the Holy Spirit." This is not a once-for-all occurrence, but something we need to do *continually*. The filling of the Spirit, then, is relying upon his indwelling influence to empower us to live like—to be like—Jesus Christ.

Three Divine Directives

There are three other New Testament commands linked with the Spirit.

First, earlier in Ephesians, Paul wrote, "Do not grieve the Holy Spirit of God, with whom you were sealed for the day of redemption" (4:30). In the context, "grieving" is done by mistreating or having bad attitudes toward other Christians. But it likewise seems correct to say that *any* form of sin—any *unholiness*—would grieve the *Holy* Spirit.

Second, Paul also says, "Do not quench the Spirit. Do not treat prophecies with contempt" (1 Thessalonians 5:19–20). Fire is a biblical symbol of power; to quench the Spirit, or put out the Spirit's fire, is to disturb his work. In the context, this is done by regarding the means by which the Spirit communicated to God's people (through prophecy) with contempt or disdain. And again, it seems correct to assume we can douse the Spirit's fire if we resist his work by any means.

These are sobering realities. We can actually bring a strong negative emotion upon the Holy Spirit (*grieve* him), and we can actually frustrate the power of omnipotent God (*quench* him)! This demonstrates sin's utter sinfulness—it shows just how seriously we should take sin.

The third command is this: "Walk by the Spirit, and you will not gratify the desires of the flesh" (Galatians 5:16). The previous verse adds the related idea, "Let us keep in step with the Spirit," that is, follow his leading.

If we obey this order, what will result? Negatively, we will not indulge the cravings of our sinful impulses. Positively, the Spirit will produce his "fruit" in the believer's life! These qualities— "love, joy, peace, forbearance, kindness, goodness, faithfulness, gentleness and self-control" (vv. 22–23)—are the Spirit's responsibility to produce, not ours. If we live (or walk) by the Spirit, he *will* produce this fruit within us.

If we are filled with the Holy Spirit, living by him and following him, we will not grieve him or quench him. Rather, he will give us the power we lack in and of ourselves to be Christlike in our actions, attitudes, and character.

INTERESTING FACT

But wait—there's more! The Spirit also reveals truth, specifically about Christ and his teachings (John 14:26; 15:26; 16:13). He assures us we really are God's children (Romans 8:16). He helps us in our weakness and prays for us when words fail us (vv. 26-27). What an amazing gift he is for believers. Let us take full advantage of all he was sent to provide for us.

What Are the Gifts of the Spirit?

In addition to his ministries surveyed in chapter 24, the Holy Spirit also gives "spiritual gifts." The Greek term *charisma* comes from the family of words related to *grace* and therefore means something like "grace gift" or "free gift." This term is used of the gift of salvation in general (e.g., Romans 6:23), but in other contexts it is used in a more specific sense of an ability given through the Holy Spirit to serve the body of Christ (the church).

For example, "God has appointed in the church, first apostles, second prophets, third teachers, then miracles, then gifts of healings, helps, administrations, various kinds of tongues" (1 Corinthians 12:28 NASB). This verse is part of the major New Testament spiritual-gifts section: 1 Corinthians 12–14. The other main texts that address this concept are Romans 12:3–8; Ephesians 4:4–13; and 1 Peter 4:10–11. And it seems these lists are best understood as representative, not exhaustive. (In other words, there are probably spiritual gifts that do not appear in them.)

These are defined as abilities given *to serve the body of Christ* because of very clear purpose statements, such as 1 Corinthians

12:7: "To each one the manifestation of the Spirit is given *for the common good*," and 14:12: "Since you are eager for gifts of the Spirit, try to excel in those that *build up the church*" (see also 14:26; Ephesians 4:15–16). The main point is that these gifts are not given for our own individual benefit and enjoyment but rather for the benefit of others corporately, namely, our brothers and sisters in Christ.

Another clearly stated truth about spiritual gifts is that God sovereignly distributes them according to his will (1 Corinthians 12:11, 18). This means God has given each and every Christian a role and responsibility in the body of Christ and the supernatural ability, in the form of a spiritual gift or gifts, to fulfill it. He knows best how to orchestrate this, and we should be content with the gifts he chooses for us.

One Matter of Debate

A significant controversy in this area has divided Christians, and especially in the last century or so. Here is the question: Does God still give certain miraculous spiritual gifts (like working miracles, healing, prophecy [relaying directly given divine revelation], and speaking in tongues [languages neither learned natively nor formally]), or were these given exclusively during the early days of the church? There are two camps in this discussion.

Cessationists believe that God ceased giving these particular gifts after the first century. As such, they were a part of what he was doing early on to authenticate the work and authority of the apostles (Hebrews 2:4–6) and through them to establish the church on its "foundation" (Ephesians 2:20–22); they are no longer necessary.

Continuationists believe that God has continued bestowing these gifts since the first century. One of their main points is that no biblical texts clearly state that these spiritual gifts were temporary and not for all the church throughout history.

A primary controversial passage is 1 Corinthians 13:8–10:

> Love never fails. But where there are prophecies, they will cease; where there are tongues, they will be stilled; where there is knowledge, it will pass away. For we know in part and we prophesy in part, but when completeness comes, what is in part disappears.

Here Paul affirms that prophecy, tongues, and knowledge (supernaturally given) will indeed cease at some point. The question is when? More specifically, what does "when completeness comes" mean?

Cessationists say this phrase either means (1) when the New Testament canon is completed and we have God's complete written revelation, or (2) when the church comes to a relative degree of "maturity" (which the Greek word translated *completeness* or *perfection* can mean), as opposed to its first-century infancy (v. 11 contrasts being a child and being a man). The Bible is complete; the church is no longer in its infancy, so these gifts are no longer needed.

Continuationists say this phrase refers to Christ's second coming. This is what Paul means in saying, "Now we see only a reflection as in a mirror; then we shall see face to face. Now I know in part; then I shall know fully, even as I am fully known" (v. 12). These gifts will cease only after Christ's return (compare 1 Corinthians 1:7).

Cessationists also say these miraculous gifts essentially disappeared from history soon after the first century, and that this is evidence that God ceased to give them. Continuationists, while acknowledging that these gifts did seem to become less evident from the second century on, say this does not mean they ceased altogether. There seems to be at least limited evidence of these gifts during various times of revival. Also, perhaps the relative laxity of the church explains the relative scarcity of such spiritual gifts.

Cessationists also have argued that when phenomena like speaking in tongues, miracles, and healing are documented in non-Christian religions, *these* certainly cannot be thought of as gifts of God. Continuationists counter that Satan's ability to counterfeit God's work and cause miracles does not mean all miraculous occurrences are counterfeits.

What Should Be Our Focus?

First, we should acknowledge that Scripture is not as clear regarding this issue as we might like it to be. For some reason, God did not see fit to answer all of our questions regarding miraculous spiritual gifts.

Second, we should realize that in the main biblical discussion of spiritual gifts—1 Corinthians 12–14—Paul is "troubleshooting," writing to correct abuses in the Corinthian church. Even spiritual gifts can be abused; for example, they can be used or exercised out of pride or for one's own glory (Romans 12:3). We are to exercise spiritual gifts in keeping with their plainly stated purpose: to build up the church as a whole, not our own reputation or ego.

Third, as in all that believers do, our motive is as important as the act itself. This is why, at the very heart of this discussion, Paul gave us the great "love chapter" (1 Corinthians 13). The point is that if *any* spiritual gifts are motivated by *anything* other than love, they amount to *nothing* (vv. 2–3).

Fourth, though Paul does not say all we might like him to say on this topic, he gives unambiguous guidelines regarding the exercise of miraculous gifts in the gathering of Christ's body (1 Corinthians 14:27–32). Churches that do practice these gifts must carefully follow this biblical guidance.

Ironically, the manner in which this controversy about the miraculous spiritual gifts has been handled—by both sides—has often been divisive, contrary to the Spirit's own work to bring unity to the church (Ephesians 4:3). Everyone needs to (and most do) acknowledge that this issue is of secondary importance. For the sake of unity, we are to be gracious in holding our convictions while accepting and loving anyone with whom we may disagree.

INTERESTING FACT

There is no command to know one's spiritual gift(s). We may or we may not; either way it shouldn't bother us. Rather, we are to be willing to serve the body of Christ in some way. God will certainly direct us to a venue of service that coincides with the spiritual gift(s) he, through his Spirit, has given us.

What Is the Basis of Salvation?

Who needs to be saved? *Everyone!* Not one person has escaped sin's devastating effects, and no one can do anything about this on their own. This was the subject of chapters 15 and 16. Finally we come to the solution to the universal problem: the doctrine of salvation.

The basis of salvation for any and every individual is Christ's death—and *only* Christ's death. This truth is known as the sufficiency of the death of Christ. Anything we sinful humans might contribute to our own salvation is excluded. When Jesus said on the cross, "It is finished" (John 19:30), he meant it. The gospel—the good news of salvation—is succinctly stated in 1 Corinthians 15:1–8:

> By this gospel you are saved . . . that *Christ died for our sins* according to the Scriptures, that he was buried, that he was raised on the third day according to the Scriptures, and that he appeared [to the disciples and hundreds of others].
>
> vv. 2–5

The good news is that anyone can be saved by believing that Jesus died for their sins, was buried, and was resurrected.

The significance of his death could be compared to a diamond with many facets. Each describes an effect of Christ's work, either on God the Father or on individuals in need of salvation.

What the Death of Christ Was

The first and central concept is known as *substitutionary atonement* (penal substitution or vicarious atonement). This has to do with what Christ's death *was*—its essence. The sinner, having broken God's law, deserves legal punishment, namely, death (Genesis 2:17; Romans 5:12; 6:23; James 1:15).

The death of Christ solves this problem in terms of atonement, which means "the making right of a wrong." When that wrong is between a human and God, atonement can only be accomplished through death (Hebrews 9:22). The terms *substitution* or *vicarious* mean the one sacrificed dies in the place of or instead of the sinner.

This concept was introduced through the Old Testament sacrificial system. For example, in Leviticus 17:11, God says, "The life of a creature is in the blood, and I have given it to you to make atonement for yourselves on the altar; it is the blood that makes atonement for one's life." But animals were never a sufficient substitute for humans, who are created in the image of God (Hebrews 10:4, 11). God provided animal sacrifices as a theology lesson regarding the seriousness of sin and the means of dealing with it, and in anticipation of what was to come.

Only one who is truly human could die in the place of another. That is why Jesus "*had to* be made like them, *fully human in every way* . . . that he might make atonement for the sins of the people*" (Hebrews 2:17). He tells us in Mark 10:45 that his death was truly a substitute: "The Son of Man did not come to be served, but to serve, and to give his life as a ransom for many." Paul says, in 1 Timothy 2:6, that Christ "gave himself as a ransom for all people."

The Greek word translated *for* in both verses specifically means "in the place of" or "instead of." Many other texts speak of the substitutionary nature of the sacrifice (e.g., Matthew 20:28; John 1:29; Romans 5:8; 2 Corinthians 5:21; Galatians 3:13; 1 Peter 3:18). The effect on God the Father of Christ's substitutionary sacrifice was that his justice—a part of his very nature—was satisfied (Romans 3:25–26). God, being holy and righteous, *did* punish sin as he *had* to do. The effect on sinners is that Christ, in our place, paid the penalty for our sin; he was punished instead of us (Isaiah 53:5; Romans 4:25). As a result, we can be purified from every sin (1 John 1:7).

What the Death of Christ Did

Whereas substitutionary atonement primarily has to do with what his death *was,* other New Testament concepts focus on what Christ's death *did.* One result is *reconciliation*, the changing of a relationship from hostility to peace. The death of Christ heals the sin-caused rift in the sinner's relationship with God; through Christ, the sinner and God are brought together (Romans 5:10–11; 2 Corinthians 5:18–20; Ephesians 2:13–16; Colossians 1:20).

Another result of Christ's death is *propitiation*. Because of sin, the sinner is under God's wrath and will ultimately experience it (Romans 1:18; 2:5, 8; Ephesians 5:6; Colossians 3:6). *Propitiation* refers to turning away wrath, and this is what Christ's death accomplished. "God displayed [Christ] publicly as a propitiation in His blood" (Romans 3:25; see also Hebrews 2:17; 1 John 2:2; 4:10 [all NASB[1]]). Through Jesus, we can be delivered from God's wrath (Romans 5:9; 1 Thessalonians 1:9–10).

Another result of Christ's death is *redemption*. This effect of what Jesus did is that sinners, slaves of sin, are set free (Romans

6:6, 16; 7:14). Sinners not only are redeemed from sin but also are rescued "from the dominion of darkness" (Colossians 1:13–14), Satan's control. Closely connected to this is that Christ's work on the cross has actually defeated Satan, demons, sin, and death (Colossians 2:13–15). And it gets even better: Believers, set free from unrighteousness, are now, blessedly, *slaves of righteousness* and of *Christ* (Romans 6:17–22; 1 Corinthians 7:22; Ephesians 1:7).

So the central idea of Christ's death as the basis for salvation is that it was a substitutionary atonement to accomplish redemption, reconciliation, and propitiation for the sinner who turns to him in faith.

Through the centuries, many have objected to this essence of Christ's death because, they say, it is abhorrent due to its violence (blood and death) and unjust due to Jesus' being completely innocent (he lived a perfect, sinless life). There is truth in both reactions. It was necessarily violent, though, because of sin's sinfulness; the seriousness of sin means it can be addressed only through serious means. Also, the objection of injustice overlooks the truth that "God made him who had no sin to be sin for us" (2 Corinthians 5:21). Jesus became sin as, by God's doing, he bore our sins and sinfulness.

Other Ideas on the Death of Christ

Some have rejected the significance of Christ's death as a *substitutionary* sacrifice and understood it in other ways. For instance, a number of early church fathers (theologians in the centuries after the first century) understood Christ's death primarily in terms of a *ransom* paid to Satan. If Satan had held sinners captive, the death of Jesus was the ransom paid to free his captives; this view was based on texts like Matthew 20:28, Mark 10:45, and 1 Timothy 2:6, which use the term *ransom* of Christ's death. However, they do not indicate who received the ransom, and more likely this is the Father himself, the one wronged by sinners, rather than Satan, who by the death of Jesus was not enriched but rather defeated.

Others have seen Christ's death as being more for the benefit of sinners than for the benefit of God himself. For example, the *moral influence* view of the atonement is that the death of Jesus demonstrated God's love for sinners. The reformed sinner's proper response to such overwhelming love is love for God in return, in the form of obedience, which results in acceptance by God. What is right here is that the cross of Christ does reveal God's love (John 3:16). The problem, though, is that human obedience can never overcome human sinfulness and result in God's acceptance (Ephesians 2:8–9).

A more extreme version of this theory has been called the *example* view. More than the death of Christ, it was his life that provides an example of righteousness and obedience for us to follow in order to be accepted by God. However, again, this assumes that sinners can make themselves acceptable to God, which Scripture clearly rejects.

INTERESTING FACT

What religion or ideology has as its symbol a notorious means of execution? The very idea sounds ludicrous. Yet Christianity's universally recognized symbol is exactly that. In this case, though, the cross, along with the empty grave, is not symbolic of death and defeat but of life and victory! "The message of the cross is foolishness to those who are perishing, but to us who are being saved it is the power of God" (1 Corinthians 1:18).

How Does God Choose Who Will Be Saved?

The question of God's choice regarding those who will be saved is a major divide between Calvinism and Arminianism (introduced in chapter 11). Notice that the question is not "*Does* God choose those who will be saved?" The Bible clearly says God chooses, or elects, those who will be saved. For example,

> He chose [or, elected] us in him before the creation of the world to be holy and blameless in his sight. In love he predestined us for adoption to sonship through Jesus Christ, in accordance with his pleasure and will.
>
> Ephesians 1:4–5

Note that *chose* and *predestined* are essentially the same in meaning here. So we are contemplating the doctrine of predestination, a subcategory of the doctrine of divine providence (see chapter 11). A common misconception is that Calvinists believe in divine election and predestination while Arminians do not. However, the Bible says God does indeed choose and predestine. The question is not *does* God elect? but *how* does God elect—on what basis?

Conditional Election

Arminians believe in *conditional* election. They hold that given God's ability to look into the future and know for certain what will happen before it happens, he knows beforehand who will believe in Jesus and be saved. Based on this "foreknowledge," he chooses them for salvation "before the creation of the world" (Ephesians 1:4). "Those God foreknew he also predestined to be conformed to the image of his Son, that he might be the firstborn among many brothers and sisters" (Romans 8:29; compare 1 Peter 1:2).

The condition, then, is the person's saving faith, which God foreknows. This fits with what we have already seen to be central to Arminian theology, that because God's love is perfect, he gives all people free will, including the ability to trust in Christ or reject Christ. Therefore, with regard to salvation, God's choice in election is based on the individual's choice regarding Christ (even though that choice has not yet been made in the flow of history).

Two key biblical texts for the Arminian view are 1 Timothy 2:4—"[God] wants all people to be saved and to come to a knowledge of the truth"—and 2 Peter 3:9—"[The Lord] is patient with you, not wanting anyone to perish, but everyone to come to repentance." Since God loves all people (John 3:16), shows no partiality (Deuteronomy 10:17; Romans 2:11), and clearly wants *all* people to be saved (see also Ezekiel 18:23, 32; 33:11), it does not make sense that he would choose some and not others for salvation apart from their decision to accept or reject Christ as Savior. It boils down to this: All people are sinners and deserve to go to hell. God loves *all* people and sent his Son to die for *all* people. As a result of God's grace given to *all* people (more on this later), *all* people are able to believe in Christ for salvation. The choice to do so is entirely up to the individual. According to Arminians, only this view makes sense of the multitude of biblical passages that invite sinners to believe and be saved (e.g., Acts 16:30–31).

Unconditional Election

Calvinists, who believe in *unconditional* election, reject any condition for God's choice outside of God himself (specifically, the individual's foreknown faith). God's choice of who will be saved is based entirely on *his* plans and purposes. No biblical text says God's choice is based on any human choice. Rather, for instance, "He predestined us for adoption to sonship through Jesus Christ, *in accordance with his pleasure and will*" (Ephesians 1:5).

What about the texts that say God chose according to his foreknowledge (Romans 8:29; 1 Peter 1:2)? Calvinists say the Greek term translated *foreknowledge* means more than just knowing about something before it happens (a concept known as *simple foreknowledge*); it means "an intimate relationship with someone before that person is even born." This is based on the biblical concept of "knowing" as more than intellectual; it includes relationship. For example, "[Adam] had relations with [literally, *knew*] his wife Eve, and she conceived and gave birth to Cain" (Genesis 4:1 NASB). A man's intellectual knowledge of a woman does not produce a baby! This is why God could say of Jeremiah, "Before I formed you in the womb I *knew* you, before you were born I set you apart" (Jeremiah 1:5). Surely this cannot just mean God had intellectual knowledge of Jeremiah before his birth. So the term *foreknowledge,* understood in this way, supports *unconditional* election.

Calvinists claim biblical support from texts like John 6, in which Jesus speaks of a "group" that the Father gives to him, draws to him, and enables to come to him (vv. 37, 39, 44, 65). Those not in this group cannot come; those in this group not only can come but do indeed come. This group seems to be what other texts refer to as the "elect" (Matthew 24:22–31; Romans 8:33). Jesus said to his disciples, "You did not choose me, but I chose you and appointed you so that you might go and bear fruit." This seems to deny the divine choice is based on any human choice (John 15:16; see also Romans 9:16 [below]).

In several passages the order is significant. In John 10:26, Jesus says, "You do not believe because you are not my sheep [the elect]." Acts 13:48 says of those who heard the gospel, "all who were appointed for eternal life [the elect] believed." In both, being one of the elect produces belief, rather than the other way around (as Arminians maintain).

Probably the strongest biblical support for *unconditional* election comes from Romans 9:1–24. Paul argues that God has the right to make his choices: "It does not, therefore, depend on human desire or effort, but on God's mercy" (v. 16). This seems to rule out God's decisions being based on anything humans want or do. The basis is within God himself, specifically his mercy.

A common criticism of this understanding of predestination is that it is unfair to base such a decision on anything but what humans freely choose. Paul addresses this: "What then shall we say? Is God unjust? Not at all!" (v. 14). Since God is the potter (the Creator), he has the right to do with the clay (his creation) as he chooses. Who are we to question his ways (vv. 19–21)?

The deep things of God are tough to understand. The complexity leads some Christians to try to avoid the whole matter.

But God has spoken about it in his Word, so we ought to be willing to consider these texts, come to our own convictions, and humbly hold to them while we remember:

> Oh, the depth of the riches of the wisdom and knowledge of God!
> How unsearchable his judgments, and his paths beyond tracing out!
>
> Romans 11:33

INTERESTING FACT

Apart from the two primary views described above, some believe that election is not individual but rather corporate. That is, God has not chosen for salvation certain individuals but a whole group. In the Old Testament era, he chose the nation of Israel for his special blessing. In the New Testament era, that chosen group is the church, Christ's body. If this is so, an individual can only be considered "elect" once he or she has believed in Jesus as Savior and been united with the body of Christ.

Did Jesus Die for Everyone?

I f the death of Jesus Christ is the only basis for one's salvation, this question must be asked: Did he die for everyone or not for everyone? Specifically, did Jesus die for all people, even people who will never believe and be saved? Or did Jesus die only for those whom God knew would eventually believe and be saved (the elect)? Arminians and Calvinists answer differently.

Unlimited Atonement

Arminians believe Jesus died for all people—the elect and the non-elect, those who will be saved and those who will never be saved. *Unlimited* (or general) atonement, the view that God sent Jesus to die for all, is consistent with Arminian theology because it stresses God's love for *all* people (John 3:16) and his desire for *all* people to be saved (1 Timothy 2:4; 2 Peter 3:9).

Obviously, the fact that he died for all does not save all people automatically; the Bible is clear that, in judgment, many sinners will be separated from God eternally. However, it does make all people *potentially* savable. The decision is left up to each individual to believe, or not to believe, in Jesus as their Savior. Only when the individual believes is the potential salvation that Jesus provided actualized for that individual.

Numerous biblical texts seem to support this view. Upon seeing Jesus, John the Baptist exclaimed, "Look, the Lamb of God, who takes away the sin of *the world!*" (John 1:29). Just after Paul says that God desires all people to be saved (1 Timothy 2:4), he adds, "[Christ] gave himself as a ransom for *all people*" (v. 6). And, a bit later in the same letter: "We have put our hope in the living God, who is the Savior of *all people,* and especially of those who believe" (4:10). "[Jesus Christ] is the atoning sacrifice for our sins, and not only for ours but also for the sins of the *whole world*" (1 John 2:2).

One theological argument for unlimited atonement is this: If Jesus did not die for all, how can the gospel be legitimately offered to all? (See John 3:14–18; Acts 17:30; Romans 10:13.) If Jesus didn't die for everyone, salvation cannot be offered to everyone.

Limited Atonement

Most Calvinists believe Jesus died only for the elect, meaning those who eventually will believe in Jesus and be saved. This view is called *limited* (or particular) atonement—limited to the elect, not limited in value or sufficiency.

There are also biblical texts that appear to support this view. Jesus said, "The Son of Man did not come to be served, but to serve, and to give his life as a ransom for *many*" (Matthew 20:28) and "This is my blood of the covenant, which is poured out for *many* for the forgiveness of sins" (Matthew 26:28). More specifically, he, the good shepherd, said, "I lay down my life for *the sheep*" (John 10:15). *Sheep* refers to those who would follow him—the elect. Similarly, Paul wrote, "Christ loved the *church* and gave himself up for *her*" (Ephesians 5:25). The church is made up of the elect.

Theologically, Calvinists argue against unlimited atonement in several ways. First, if Jesus died for all people, then why aren't all people saved? Why doesn't this view result in universalism? Second, if Jesus died for all people but not all are saved as a result, doesn't this mean Jesus failed in his work on the cross? Isn't some of the value of his death wasted on those who do not believe? Third, if Jesus died for all people and yet those who do not believe are sent to hell as punishment for their sins, doesn't that amount to two punishments for the same sin? Even we humans have laws against double jeopardy. Doesn't this imply that God is unjust?

A "Third View"

In this case, a mediating position that seems to make the most sense comes from recognizing that God was doing more through the death of Jesus than providing the basis of salvation. There is truth in both of the first two positions, so the third view can be stated like this: Jesus did indeed die for all people, but especially for the elect.

This seems to be exactly Paul's point in saying Jesus "is the Savior of all people, and especially of those who believe" (1 Timothy 4:10). John makes the same point: "[Jesus] is the atoning sacrifice for [believers'] our sins, and not only for ours but also for the sins of the whole world" (1 John 2:2).

An important question to consider here is "How did the apostle John use the term *world*, in this text and in others (e.g., John 3:16; 1 John 5:19)?" A word study indicates that not only is he talking about all people in the world, but he is also including the additional idea that all people are bad. In John's usage, *world* often has a morally negative connotation, referring to all people who are in rebellion against God (e.g.,

1 John 2:15–17; 3:13; 5:4–5). This is clearly seen in 1 John 5:19, "The whole world [same phrase as in 2:2] is under the control of the evil one." This supports the notion that Jesus really did die for all people—all *evil* people—and emphasizes God's love for all.

In Paul's words, "God demonstrates his own love for us in this: While we were still sinners, Christ died for us" (Romans 5:8). It's even more amazing to consider that, knowing those who would reject and even hate Christ to the very end of their life, he still died specifically for them. One divine purpose in the atonement is *to magnify God's amazing love for all people.*

Jesus died for *all*. *All* are invited to Christ, and *all* who come and believe will be saved. We truly can say to anyone, "Jesus died for *you*." So another purpose in the atonement was *to provide a basis for the universal offer of the gospel and the provisional salvation of all.*

But it also seems to be true that knowing who the elect are, Jesus died for them in a special way in order to secure their salvation, thus the texts cited above regarding Jesus dying for the "many," the "sheep," and his "church." Though God loves all people, he has a more intense love for his own. This was true of his Old Testament people, Israel (see Deuteronomy 10:15). He loved Egyptians and Canaanites, but he loved Israel in a more focused way. Now that love is also focused on the church (see Ephesians 5:25). So yet another purpose in the atonement was *to secure the salvation of the elect.*

Another way to state this mediating position is this: The atonement was *sufficient* for all and *efficient* for the elect. It was sufficient for all in that Jesus' death for all renders all people potentially savable if they will only believe. It was efficient for the elect in that the elect will believe, thus turning their salvation from potential to actual.[1]

INTERESTING FACT

Dr. Bruce Ware, professor of theology at Southern Baptist Theological Seminary, calls this mediating view *Un/limited atonement*. This term captures the validity within both the limited and unlimited atonement views.

How Does a Person Become Saved?

Even though the salvation of any individual happens instantaneously, there is a process that can be traced based on New Testament words and concepts. Theologians call this the *ordo salutis,* or order of salvation.

Conviction. This term refers to the act of showing someone their faults. It is used, for example, in Matthew 18:15: "If your brother or sister sins, go and point out their fault, just between the two of you." With regard to salvation, this is the work of the Holy Spirit (John 16:8–11). Only the Spirit can effectively reveal the sinful state of any person, and apart from this no one will even feel the need for salvation.

Calling. The contexts in which this Greek word is used indicate two types of calling, or invitation. One, the "general call," is the universal offer of the gospel to all people, the invitation to everyone to believe in Jesus and receive salvation. For example, Jesus said, "Many are invited, but few are chosen" (Matthew

22:14). Luke 14:16–24 records the parable of the man who invited many to a dinner, but some offered excuses regarding why they could not come. These texts indicate that while the invitation to salvation goes to all, not all accept it. This type of divine invitation can be declined.

In other texts, those who receive the invitation do accept it. This second type is the "effectual call" or "effective call." Paul addresses 1 Corinthians to "saints by calling" (1:2 NASB) and refers to "those whom God has called" (1:24), expressions essentially equivalent to "Christians" or "the elect." Paul also says, "Those [God] predestined, he also called" (Romans 8:30). This type of call goes only to the elect and does result in salvation.

Divine Grace. As we have seen, sinners are spiritually dead in their sin, totally helpless, unable to do anything spiritual, especially believe in order to be saved (Romans 8:7–8). Therefore, God must enable them to do this by his grace. Calvinists and Arminians agree on this but understand necessary grace in different ways.

Arminians refer to "prevenient grace," that is, grace that precedes (comes before) saving faith. Sometimes called "enabling grace," it enables spiritually dead people to do what they would otherwise not be able to do. Also, Arminians believe God gives this type of divine grace to *everyone* in order to overcome the effects of sin, but it is also resistible. That is, because of free will, not everyone exercises this God-given ability, and some decline the general call to be saved.

Calvinists prefer to speak of what has historically been called *irresistible grace*. The term unfortunately smacks of compulsion; it sounds like, through this kind of grace, God forces the elect to believe in the gospel. But this is *not* what Calvinists believe. Rather, they hold that this type of grace is given only to the elect (not to all people), and it does indeed result in the elect exercising saving faith, through compelling persuasion (not coercive pressure).

The conversion of Saul/Paul (Acts 9) is an illustration. As a loyal Jew, Saul hated Jesus Christ and his followers and was on his way to Damascus to arrest some of them. But when he was confronted by the resurrected, glorified Christ, it immediately became obvious that what he had believed to be a lie was undeniably true: Jesus was the promised Messiah, and he was very much alive. As a result, Paul believed. Jesus did not force him; he just opened Paul's sin-blinded eyes to reality, and then Paul willingly and gladly believed. Paul himself describes this experience in 2 Corinthians 4:4–6.

Calvinists say this is what Jesus meant when he said, "No one can come to me unless the Father who sent me draws them" (John 6:44). Acts 16:14 records of a woman named Lydia that "the Lord opened her heart to respond to Paul's message."

Most important here is what Arminians and Calvinists both agree on: No one can be saved apart from the grace of God. Therefore, God gets all the glory and credit for the salvation of all who believe (Ephesians 1:6–12; 2:8–9).

Repentance. This concept is often misunderstood as an effort to clean up one's spiritual and moral act, but this is *not* what the Bible means by *repentance*. Rather, the Greek word literally means "to change one's mind" (or "thinking") about something. In terms of being saved, then, it means someone now thinks differently about themselves as a sinner and their absolute need of God's grace through Jesus the Savior. In this sense, repentance is really a corollary of saving faith. We can't truly repent without believing, and we can't truly believe without repenting.

Saving faith. The last step to individual salvation is the exercise of saving faith. Scripture states this repeatedly and clearly: There is no salvation apart from faith (John 3:15–16; Romans 10:9–10; Ephesians 2:8). I add *saving* here because not all faith results in salvation, as the parable of the sower illustrates. Some of the seed (the gospel) falls on rocky soil—"They believe for a while, but in the time of testing they fall away" (Luke 8:13).

Saving faith is made up of three components, and all are necessary.

First, there must be *knowledge*. This has to do with ideas or concepts generally, and specifically, knowledge of the gospel (1 Corinthians 15:3–8). No one can be saved apart from knowing the gospel.

Second, there must be *assent*. One must know what the gospel is and believe it is true (this is where repentance comes in). We all know certain concepts or stories to which we do not give assent (Santa Claus, the tooth fairy, the Easter bunny). Many people know what the gospel is yet don't believe it to be true. They are certainly not saved.

But knowledge and assent alone are not enough. Even Satan and his demons know the gospel and believe that it is true; they are certainly not saved. So finally, there must be *trust* (reliance, dependence). We not only must know what the gospel is and believe that the gospel is true, we also must completely depend upon Jesus Christ and nothing else (only the gospel—not ourselves or anyone/anything else) to make us right with God.

That's why this kind of faith and our works are always mutually exclusive in Scripture (Romans 3:21–28; Galatians 2:16; Ephesians 2:8–9). Our works do not and cannot impress God. Rather, what pleases him is our trust in and dependence upon him (Hebrews 11:6). Only when we believe the gospel and depend upon Christ in this way are we truly saved.

INTERESTING FACT

Regeneration fits in here somewhere, but not all agree where. The Greek word translated *regeneration* (e.g., NASB) is found only in

Matthew 19:28 and Titus 3:5, but the concept is that of being "reborn," "born again," or "born of God" (John 3:3; 1 John 2:29; 3:9; 4:7; 5:1, 4, 18). By the work of God through his Spirit (John 3:5-8) and his Word (1 Peter 1:23), those who were dead in sin are now spiritually and eternally alive. Arminians believe regeneration is a result of salvation—that a person is *first* saved by faith and *then* born again as a gift of God (see chapter 29). Most Calvinists believe regeneration precedes saving faith because it is a means by which God enables spiritually dead people to believe—by giving them spiritual life first.

What Are the Results of Being Saved?

The Bible calls salvation a gift (Ephesians 2:8), and salvation contains many aspects; it's a gift box full of all sorts of wonderful things. We have already seen some—for example, all the ministries of the Holy Spirit for Christians (indwelling, filling, spiritual gifts). Here are just a few of the many more:

Forgiveness. Probably the most well-known benefit of salvation, but precious nonetheless, is forgiveness of sin (Ephesians 1:7; Colossians 2:13). Even though we have wronged God in so many ways, because Jesus paid the legal penalty for our sins, God's gracious forgiveness of them brings us from a negative moral condition to a neutral moral condition. This is phenomenal in and of itself, and it gets even better, which brings us to salvation's next result.

Justification. This legal concept means "a declaration of righteousness." Picture a courtroom in which you, the sinner, stand before God, the judge, and due to your faith in Christ, he slams down his gavel and declares, "Not guilty—righteous!" Paul unpacks this truth in Romans 3:20–31, where he makes clear this is based on God's grace demonstrated through the sacrificial death of Jesus (vv. 24–25) and happens when the sinner believes (vv. 22, 25–28). Declaring a guilty sinner "not guilty" is not a perversion of justice. Rather, God shows himself to be just (vv. 25–26) because he does punish sins—Jesus bore them and died on the cross in our place.

Having satisfied his justice, God is free in grace to justify believers. This includes forgiveness, but beyond leaving believers morally neutral, God grants them a positive standing, thus the declaration of *righteousness*. How? By God giving us his righteousness (v. 22), through *imputation*, which refers to a transfer: "God made [Christ] who had no sin to be sin for us, so that in him we might become the righteousness of God" (2 Corinthians 5:21).

In Christ, believers become God's righteousness. What an unspeakably great deal: Jesus gets our sin; we get his righteousness. The result is that when God looks at Christians, he sees not just forgiven people but also righteous people. Another vital result of this is that we are at peace with God (Romans 5:1). Only righteous people can be accepted by a righteous God.

Sanctification. The term *sanctify* literally means "to set apart," so sanctification means "setting apart to holiness" or "making righteous." This is similar to justification, but builds on it. Even after justification, sin continues to dwell in the Christian. Sanctification refers to the ongoing work (mostly God's) to rid the Christian completely of that sin, once and for all.

Various New Testament contexts reveal three tenses and types. There is a past-tense sanctification (closest to justification) usually called *positional*, which results in God seeing us as righteous (1 Corinthians 6:11; Hebrews 10:10, 14). We become "saints"—a form of the word *sanctify* that means "holy ones" (1 Corinthians 1:2)—instantaneously when we trust in Christ.

A future-tense sanctification, referred to as *perfect* or *complete*, takes place at the end of life when we stand in Christ's presence and all remaining sinfulness is removed forever (1 Thessalonians 3:13; 5:23). The Bible also uses the term *glorification* for this (Romans 8:30; 9:23).

In between, there is a present-tense sanctification known as *progressive*, because our holiness progresses as we grow in Christ and sin less. It is also called *experiential*, for we can experience or sense it as we grow in him (2 Corinthians 3:18; 4:16; 7:1). We will never become sinless in this present life, but we can sin less, with God's help. While past and future sanctification are entirely works of God, progressive sanctification is a cooperative effort between him and the believer. This is where all biblical commands to Christians come in. When we faithfully obey them in dependence upon God, we contribute to our progressive sanctification; we mature in Christ.

Freedom from the power of sin. This is a part of what makes progressive sanctification possible. Paul describes it in Romans 6: Before salvation, we are slaves of sin, which means we must obey sin; we can do nothing but sin. But when we believed, we died with Christ—died to sin's absolute control—and are now free to live holy lives (vv. 6–7). Sin still dwells within us and tries to exert control, but now, once again, we are commanded,

Count yourselves dead to sin but alive to God in Christ Jesus. Therefore do not let sin reign in your mortal body so that you obey its evil desires. Do not offer any part of yourself to sin as an instrument of wickedness, but rather offer yourselves to God as those who have been brought from death to life; and offer every part of yourself to him as an instrument of righteousness.

vv. 11–13

Being "in Christ" and having Christ in us. These concepts, favorites of the apostle Paul, are amazing realities. Christians are placed "in Christ" (Romans 8:1; 1 Corinthians 1:30; Ephesians 2:6), which implies that God sees us and treats us as he does his own Son. And not only are we in Christ, but Christ also is in us (Romans 8:8–10; 2 Corinthians 13:5; Ephesians 3:17). This makes it possible for us to live like him, to be Christlike.

Adoption. Believers become God's own sons and daughters (Romans 8:15–16; Galatians 4:4–7; Ephesians 1:5)! Not only is God our King, because we are in his kingdom, he is also our Father, because we are in his family.

Inheritance. Because we are in God's family, we are heirs to all that is his and have an inheritance (Galatians 4:7; Ephesians 1:14, 18; 1 Peter 1:3–4), which we share with Jesus Christ (Romans 8:17). This means there is more to the gift of salvation than what we enjoy instantly after we trust in Christ as our Savior or even throughout the rest of our lives on this earth. We also will enjoy the complete package in the presence of our Savior. That brings us to the next result of salvation.

Hope. Christians are given hope in Christ (Romans 8:20–25; Ephesians 1:18; Colossians 1:5; Titus 1:2), which means something different from how we often use the term. (I *hope* to be a professional basketball player one day [even though I'm in my fifties].) Biblical hope is a *confident assurance* that what God has promised to us in Christ (our inheritance) will *most certainly* be our possession (in the future). Hope is basically future-oriented faith. This includes the completion of our salvation and sanctification (see above). It also includes Christ's return, our resurrection, eternity in the very presence of our God, enjoying his blessings forever, and so much more. For believers, the best is indeed yet to come.

INTERESTING FACT

In chapter 29, we noted that good works have nothing to do with *becoming* a Christian (salvation is by faith alone). But good works have much to do with *being* a Christian. They likewise are a necessary result of salvation (Ephesians 2:10; Titus 2:14; 3:8). Believers do not disparage good works; they just get them in the right order—flowing from salvation, not contributing to it.

Can Christians
Lose Their Salvation?

Another theological issue to consider regarding salvation, and another significant divide between Arminianism and Calvinism, concerns *eternal security*, sometimes called *perseverance of the saints*: Can a true believer lose their salvation? Or is that person eternally secure in salvation?

There is such a thing as a "professing Christian"—someone who professes Christianity but does not truly believe in Christ (Matthew 7:22–23; Titus 1:16). There is certainly no security in salvation for that person, since they are not actually saved in the first place. Only God can know with certainty who is a true Christian, but for the sake of our discussion, we will assume that this individual is a true Christian.

Generally, one's answer to the question of whether salvation can be lost will go along with one's view of election. If election is *conditional*, then there can be no eternal security because a true Christian may cease to believe in the gospel and thus lose their salvation. So Arminians generally reject eternal security, because saints *may or may not* persevere in their faith. Some Arminians also say a true Christian can sin so significantly (e.g., the "unforgiveable sin" [see Matthew 12:31]) that they lose their salvation. This side says true Christians can lose their salvation by ceasing to believe or through significant, ongoing, unconfessed sin.

If election is *unconditional,* then eternal security makes sense, since God chose the elect according to his plans and purposes, and once they believe in the gospel, God will faithfully work to preserve them in belief and salvation. Thus Calvinists affirm eternal security; saints *will* persevere in their faith because God will enable them to do so.

Could We Be Lost?

Some biblical texts seem to argue *against* eternal security. In John 15:1–6, Jesus said any branch that does not bear fruit is removed from the vine (Jesus himself) and burned. If the "branches" are true Christians, then this sounds like the loss of salvation.

Paul says God will present us "holy in his sight, without blemish and free from accusation—if [we] continue in [our] faith, established and firm, and do not move from the hope held out in the gospel" (Colossians 1:22–23). The conditional *if* seems to suggest that we may not continue in faith and therefore would cease to be saved.

Hebrews contains a number of "warning passages" that could be understood as arguing against eternal security. Probably the most difficult (for those who believe in eternal security) is 6:4–6:

It is impossible for those who have once been enlightened, who have tasted the heavenly gift, who have shared in the Holy Spirit, who have tasted the goodness of the word of God and the powers of the coming age and who have fallen away, to be brought back to repentance.

If those referred to in verses 5 and 6 are true Christians, then it is possible for them to "fall away."

Finally, 1 Timothy 1:19–20 and 2 Timothy 2:17–18 may refer to examples of Christians who did indeed fall away.

How Could We Be Lost?

But many texts seem to argue for eternal security. Jesus said,

> I shall lose *none* of all those [my Father] has given me, but raise them up at the last day. For my Father's will is that *everyone* who looks to the Son and believes in him *shall* have eternal life, and I *will* raise them up at the last day.
>
> John 6:39–40

The reference to "eternal life" also argues for eternal security. If true Christians have eternal life (they do—1 John 5:13), how can it be lost? If it could, then it wasn't eternal in the first place, only temporary. Jesus also said,

> I give them eternal life, and they shall never perish; no one will snatch them out of my hand. My Father, who has given them to me, is greater than all; no one can snatch them out of my Father's hand.
>
> John 10:28–29

In addition to Christians being *firmly* held in the hands of God, note that the phrase *never perish* is the strongest possible way in the Greek language to deny this possibility: "They will never, *never*, NEVER perish!"

Paul wrote, "[I am] confident of this, that [God] who began a good work in you will carry it on to completion until the day of Christ Jesus" (Philippians 1:6). The "good work" is salvation, and "the day of Christ Jesus" is his return, so it seems Paul was convinced of eternal security. Other texts also seem to say that God is committed to securing believers in Jesus in their salvation (Hebrews 7:25; Jude 24).

Paul likewise says, "God's gifts and his call are irrevocable" (Romans 11:29). Salvation is both a gift and calling of God, and therefore salvation would be irrevocable. Also, if salvation is truly a gift and therefore free (no strings attached), how might it possibly be withdrawn? If it could, it wouldn't have been a *free*, no-strings gift in the first place.

There are also theological arguments to consider. As we saw in chapter 29, the sealing of the Spirit (Ephesians 4:30) seems to indicate eternal security. Also, the possibility of losing salvation due to any sin at all seems contrary to the clear biblical teaching regarding salvation by grace *apart from works*. If works have nothing to do with our salvation in the first place, how can works (in this case, sin) have anything to do with losing it? Further, the possibility of losing salvation due to sin seems to call into question the sufficiency of Christ's death for *all* sin. If he died for *all* sin, then believers are forgiven of *all* sin, and no sin can ever jeopardize our salvation.

Again, those who reject eternal security believe a true Christian can cease to believe in the gospel and thus lose their salvation. But if saving faith is a gift of God (Ephesians 2:8–9; most Arminians agree), it seems this gift would be sufficient for the purpose given (salvation) and would never fail. In other words, God would enable Christians to persevere in their faith. He would not give a gift that in the end would not achieve its intended result.

HEARTFELT ATTEMPT TO PERSUADE

Even though I have tried to mute my own theological convictions as I write, I would wish to convince you of the truth of eternal security. I wish this not only because I do think it is true and biblical but also because I think it is God's desire for us. It would break my heart if my daughter, Kimberly, lived in fear of doing something so bad that I would disown her. In the same way, I believe, God's heart is broken if any of his children live in such fear. His desire is for his children to live securely and confidently in their relationship with him—not because of *their* ability to maintain it but because of his.

Is Jesus the Only Way to Be Saved?

A common question asked of (and by) Christians is "What about those who have never heard the gospel? Can they be saved? Or is Jesus the only way?"

Both universalism—which says all people will eventually be saved—and pluralism—which says there are many ways to God—say Jesus is *not* the only way to salvation. However, Scripture clearly and consistently says many will be eternally separated from God under divine judgment (Matthew 7:13; Revelation 20:15), and also condemns religions that reject him (Exodus 20:3–5; Isaiah 31:7; 1 Corinthians 10:7; 12:2). Neither universalism nor pluralism can be true.

Exclusivism and Inclusivism

The two views held by evangelicals are exclusivism and inclusivism. Exclusivists (restrictivists) say, "Only those who have heard the gospel and believe in Jesus as their Savior can be saved." Inclusivists say, "Jesus is the only way to be saved, but it is possible for those who have never heard the gospel and do not know Christ to be accepted by God and brought into his family."

Exclusivism, the traditional and majority view, is supported by texts like John 14:6: Jesus himself said, "I am the way and the truth and the life. No one comes to the Father except through me." In Acts 4:12, Peter said to the Jewish religious leaders, "Salvation is found in no one else, for there is no other name under heaven given to mankind by which we must be saved." Stated negatively, "Whoever does not believe stands condemned already because they have not believed in the name of God's one and only Son" (John 3:18).

After quoting Joel 2:32, "Everyone who calls on the name of the LORD will be saved" (Romans 10:13), Paul asks, "How, then, can they call on the one they have not believed in? And how can they believe in the one of whom they have not heard? And how can they hear without someone preaching to them?" (v. 14). He seems to assume the necessity of *hearing* the gospel in order to be saved. If inclusivism is right and there can be salvation apart from the gospel, then according to exclusivists, there is no motivation for evangelism. In fact, if inclusivism is correct, we may actually jeopardize the salvation of many people by proclaiming the gospel to them, because if they do hear it and then reject it, they are most certainly lost forever (John 3:18). Either way, according to exclusivists, inclusivism hinders the work of missions.

Inclusivism says salvation is possible through belief in general revelation apart from special revelation—specifically, knowledge of Christ and his work of atonement. However, exclusivists point out that Paul says even though God has clearly revealed himself in creation (general revelation), for example, *everyone* has rejected this knowledge (Romans 1:18–25). A bit later, he strings together quotations from the Psalms and says,

There is *no one* righteous, *not even one*;
there is *no one* who understands,
there is *no one* who seeks God.
All have turned away,
they have together become worthless;
there is *no one* who does good,
not even one.

Romans 3:10–12

Such universal language seems to deny the possibility that inclusivism assumes. *No one* has been drawn to God through general revelation; *all* people "suppress the truth by their wickedness" (1:18). So the *only* way to be right with God is through special revelation.

We Can Count on God's Justice

Contrary to the accusations of some critics, exclusivists do *not* believe God holds people accountable for what they have never heard, namely, special revelation—Jesus Christ and his gospel. Rather, he holds people accountable for what they do know, whether it is general or special revelation. God is just and will judge all people justly.

The exclusivist view is not easy to hold, and it has been much criticized because it denies hope of salvation for anyone throughout history who has never heard of Jesus Christ. Exclusivists emphasize, though, that we should embrace theological beliefs not because they make us feel good or make sense to our small minds but because they best represent what the Bible says.

Exclusivism and inclusivism *agree* that no one can be saved apart from Christ's death for sin and that there is only one Savior (John 14:6; Acts 4:12). But inclusivists also say this does *not* mean the only way to be saved is by first hearing the gospel and then trusting in Jesus as Savior.

While nearly all Calvinists and most Arminians hold to exclusivism, some Arminians argue for inclusivism. To them, it just does not make sense that God, who is love (1 John 4:8, 16), loves all people (John 3:16), and wants all to be saved (1 Timothy 2:4; 2 Peter 3:9)—all central Arminian tenets—would only accept the ones throughout history who have heard the gospel of Jesus Christ and believed specifically in him. Certainly he accepts others who do the best possible with what limited knowledge they have through general revelation. In other words, if those who have never heard the gospel still do believe in the Creator and Provider of all things and truly want to know him, God will accept them. After all, as Paul said to pagans, "God did [what he did among the nations] so that they would seek him and perhaps reach out for him and find him, though he is not far from any one of us" (Acts 17:27).

Or, if those who have never heard the gospel sincerely practice their non-Christian faith and do their best morally, God will accept them. After all, "It is not those who hear the law who are righteous in God's sight, but it is those who obey the law who will be declared righteous" (Romans 2:13); even pagans "show that the requirements of the law are written on their hearts" (v. 15). Inclusivists say these are the kinds of situations that can result in salvation by Christ apart from specifically believing in him. Some inclusivists call such people "anonymous Christians." They are believers but they don't even know it themselves; only God does.

Inclusivists would also point out that many have been accepted by God without knowing Christ, namely, Old Testament saints—Abraham, Moses, David, even Gentiles such as Melchizedek (Genesis 14:18–20) and Rahab (Joshua 2:8–13; Hebrews 11:31; James 2:25). If it was possible for them, couldn't it be possible for others?

This is a challenging issue. Most of us want as many people to be saved as possible. As always, the bottom line is, what does the Bible say?

INTERESTING FACT

C. S. Lewis illustrated his inclusivist belief in *The Last Battle*. In chapter 15, Aslan, the story's Christ-figure, confronts Emeth, a devoted worshiper of Tash. After Emeth admits to serving the false god, Aslan says, "Child, all the service thou hast done to Tash, I account as service done to me. . . . Therefore if any man swear by Tash and keep his oath for the oath's sake, it is by me that he has truly sworn, though he know it not, and it is I who reward him." When Emeth admits to seeking Tash his entire life, Aslan replies, "Beloved, unless thy desire had been for me thou wouldst not have sought so long and so truly. For all find what they truly seek."

What Is the Church?

Christianity in the United States often has been individualistic—"just between that person and God." While an individual relationship with God through Jesus Christ is essential, the New Testament also strongly emphasizes the corporate nature of Christianity; God is building a group of people who will glorify him and live with him forever. This group is called the church.

The English word *church* comes from the Greek term that means "of the Lord." The New Testament Greek word often translated *church* is *ekklēsia*, which means "assembly" or "gathering" (literally, "called out"). This is used in two different ways, as determined by context.

"Church": Two Meanings

First, *ekklēsia* can refer to those who profess to believe in and follow Jesus and who meet together in a specific geographical location. Paul addressed certain letters, for example, "To the church of God in Corinth" (1 Corinthians 1:2; 2 Corinthians 1:1). Near the end of his letter to the Romans, Paul said, "Greet also the church that meets at [Priscilla and Aquila's] house" (16:5; see also 1 Corinthians 16:19; Colossians 4:15). From these texts come the theological terms *local church* or *visible church*—the latter meaning that if you went to that particular location, you could see those Christians.

Second, *ekklēsia* can refer to all true Christians in all times and places. For example, "Do not cause anyone to stumble, whether Jews, Greeks or the church of God" (1 Corinthians 10:32); "God placed all things under [Christ's] feet and appointed him to be head over everything for the church" (Ephesians 1:22). These references, more cosmic in nature, go beyond a relatively few professing Christians in a certain place. From these texts come the theological terms *universal church* or *invisible church*—the latter meaning that these people are scattered through the centuries, around the world, and even in heaven, and therefore cannot be seen together (yet!).

We must note here that according to the New Testament, the church is not a place (such as a building), but a people.

The birthday of the church (in both of these senses) seems to be the day of Pentecost, as recorded in Acts 2. The argument goes like this: In Matthew 16:18, Jesus predicted and promised something to come: "I will build my church." From Ephesians 1:22–23, we know the (universal) church is the "body." From 1 Corinthians 12:13, we know all Christians are "baptized by one Spirit so as to form one body [the church]." And from Acts 11:15–16, we know Peter identified Jesus' near-future promise of the Spirit's baptism (Acts 1:5) with what occurred on the day of Pentecost. The group of people gathered in the upper room on that day became something new. The church did not exist in the Old Testament. It could come into existence only after the successful completion of Christ's messianic mission.

Illustrations and Analogies

A number of New Testament metaphors help us to understand the church's nature and importance. Most dominant is that the church is a body and Christ is its head (Romans 12:3–8; 1 Corinthians 12; Ephesians 1:22–23; 4:4–16; Colossians 1:18; 2:19). This beautifully emphasizes three truths.

First, there is *unity* among these people. Just as the physical body is one unit, so the church is one body (1 Corinthians 12:12). This oneness is based on being united to the head, Jesus Christ, and is accomplished by the work of the Holy Spirit (Ephesians 4:3).

Second, there is *diversity* within the one body. Just as the physical body's many parts do different things, so the church has many parts, namely, individual believers with different roles and responsibilities (Romans 12:4; 1 Corinthians 12:12, 14).

Third, there is *interdependence* among the many members of the one body. Just as the physical body depends upon the working of all its parts, and each part depends upon the working of other parts, so the church needs all Christians to contribute what God has called and gifted them to contribute. This is the only way the church can be built up (edified), healthy, and mature (Romans 12:5; 1 Corinthians 12:12–26; Ephesians 4:11–16; Colossians 2:19).

Jesus described the church as his flock and himself as the Good Shepherd (John 10:11–30). He cares for, protects, feeds, and nurtures his followers. He has also appointed under-shepherds to help him care for his sheep (Acts 20:28; 1 Peter 5:3). We will discuss these leaders in chapter 34.

Peter says the church is a "holy priesthood" (1 Peter 2:5–9). In contrast to the Old Testament system in which only certain people—priests in Aaron's line—could function as priests and come into God's presence, now all believers have the privilege of functioning as priests and coming directly into the presence of God through our high priest, Jesus (Hebrews 4:14–16).

Paul used three "church metaphors" in his letter to the church in Ephesus.

First, he refers to all Christians as "members of [God's] household" or family (Ephesians 2:19). He continues this image in 1 Timothy 3:15, commanding Timothy, in his pastoral role, to deal with Christians as he would his own father, mother, and siblings (1 Timothy 5:1–16; see also Titus 2:1–15). We then ought to regard fellow believers as brothers and sisters in Christ (Matthew 12:46–50) and treat them as family members.

Second, Paul refers to the church as a building (Ephesians 2:20–23; see also 1 Peter 2:5). Jesus Christ is the cornerstone, the apostles and prophets make up the rest of the foundation, and all Christians make up the building blocks of the rest of the structure. Specifically, this building is a temple in which God himself lives through the Spirit.

Third, Paul calls the church the bride and Christ the husband (Ephesians 5:23–33). The focus is on Christ's love for his bride (v. 25), his commitment to present a holy bride to himself (vv. 26–27), and the bride's responsibility to submit to his leadership (v. 24). As Paul points out, marriage between a man and a woman is patterned after and should reflect this mysterious reality.

The church is a precious gift of God to Christians and is absolutely essential to our spiritual health—both individually and corporately.

INTERESTING FACT

The pattern of ancient Near-Eastern weddings provides an analogy for the church as Christ's bride. First came a period of engagement, which, unlike today, was a legally binding agreement (a divorce was necessary to break it). This describes our relationship to Jesus right now and indicates the relationship's security. During this period, the husband-to-be prepared the house to which he would take his bride after the wedding. Jesus said he was going away to prepare a place for us; he will eventually come back to take us there to be with him forever (John 14:1–3). On the day of the wedding, the groom came with fanfare and celebration to the house of his bride-to-be. Finally, the marriage ceremony took place, followed by the marriage banquet. The church's marriage to Jesus and the marriage banquet are described in Revelation 19:7–9. Believers now are in the engagement period; we await the coming of our bridegroom, Jesus, to whom we will be eternally wedded.

How Is the Local Church to Be Governed and Led?

Even though the Bible does address the issue of leadership in the local church, there have been quite a variety of interpretations and applications of these texts down through the centuries.

Local Church Government

Historically, there have been three ways of structuring the government of the local church. The main distinction is where authority is vested.

First, *episcopal church government* is practiced, for example, in the Roman Catholic Church, Episcopalian churches, and Methodist churches. The name comes from the Greek word *episkopos*, which means "overseer." In older translations, such as the King James Version, it was rendered as *bishop*. These churches and denominations have a hierarchical structure with authority being vested in a bishop, who oversees many local churches in a certain area or diocese.

An argument for this governance form, whose history goes back to the second century, is that it duplicates what the apostles did in the first century in terms of overseeing and pastoring groups of churches in an area. An argument against it may be that *episkopos,* as used in the New Testament, is a synonym for a local church elder, not an official with authority over many churches.

Second, *congregational church government* is practiced, for example, by Congregational and Baptist churches. This approach is very democratic; authority is vested in every local church member in that each has a vote regarding church issues and offices. Another normally associated concept is that of local church autonomy, the belief that nothing outside the church (e.g., a bishop or denominational officials) has authority over any local church.

The biblical argument for this approach is the priesthood of all believers (1 Peter 2:5), thus *all* believers ought to have a say in church matters, and New Testament texts that show *all* people associated with a church involved in some issue or activity (e.g., Acts 6:1–6; 15:22; 2 Corinthians 2:6–7). A challenge is that while these texts may demonstrate *involvement* of all church members, they do not necessarily support *authority* in all members.

Third, *presbyterian church government* is practiced, for example, by Presbyterian and Reformed churches. The term comes from the Greek word *presbuteros,* which means "elder." Authority is vested in elders, individuals who are selected from within the local church. This is sometimes called *federal* church government, since the elders have the role of representing all the members. Biblical support is found in the many New Testament references to elders (e.g., Acts 11:30; 20:17; 1 Timothy 5:17; Titus 1:5; Hebrews 13:17; 1 Peter 5:1–2).

Local Church Offices

The New Testament discusses only two local church offices to which individuals are appointed: elder and deacon.

As noted above, there are many references to elders (*presbuteros*) in the local church, and this clearly is its highest level of human authority under Jesus Christ, who is head of the church. The term *episkopos* is also applied to those who hold this office since they are responsible to "oversee" the church (Acts 20:28; Philippians 1:1; 1 Timothy 3:1–2; Titus 1:7). A third term applied to this office is the verb *poimainō*, which means "to shepherd" (Acts 20:28; 1 Peter 5:2), and the noun *poimēn* (Ephesians 4:11), which refers to a shepherd and is often translated *pastor*. This too illustrates a key responsibility of elders—to shepherd the flock of Christ. The main point here is that these are different terms that refer to one office, not three.

Unfortunately, through the centuries, three *offices* have often been derived from these terms. *Overseers* or *bishops* have been understood to be in authority over groups of churches. *Pastors* have been understood to be paid church leaders formally educated in the Bible and pastoral ministry. And *elders* have been understood as local church lay-leaders who have vocations other than ministry but also hold an office of leadership in the church. But the New Testament does *not* make these distinctions. The three terms are three ways of referring to those who hold one office: *elder* = *overseer* = *pastor*.

It is noteworthy that the New Testament always refers to *elders* in the plural. This seems to assume this office is to be held by multiple individuals, not just one. That makes sense in that it guards against abuse of power invested in one person and balances the strengths and weaknesses of multiple leaders for the welfare of the church. These multiple elders are equal in authority but may have different responsibilities (as 1 Timothy 5:17 demonstrates).

Those who hold this office are to be qualified according to lists of traits Paul gives in 1 Timothy 3:1–7 and Titus 1:5–9. The emphasis is on *character*, not skills. Two skills are listed: teaching and ability to manage one's household; both are absolutely necessary for church leaders. What is stressed, though, is not one's ability, but one's character—local church elders need to be godly, Christlike, spiritually mature.

Basically, the functions of elders are to provide general leadership in the church, to teach biblical truth verbally as well as through lifestyle (Hebrews 13:7), to protect the church from doctrinal error and false teaching (Acts 20:28ff), and to make sure the church's general needs are met (Acts 20:28; 1 Peter 5:2).

The only other New Testament local church office is *deacon*. The term comes from the Greek word *diakonos,* which means "servant" or "minister." The word's only occurrences in the technical sense of those who hold this office are in Philippians 1:1 and 1 Timothy 3:8–13. The office's origin seems to be seen in Acts 6:1–6, where the Jerusalem church's elders/pastors appointed a number of men to oversee a particular task (equitable distribution of food) so that the elders themselves could keep their priorities of "prayer and the ministry of the word" (v. 4). If this is the prototype of the deacon's office, then the deacon's function seems to be with regard to the church's *material* and *physical* needs in order to assist and support the elders by allowing them to keep their highest priorities—meeting its *spiritual* needs.

Recently a hot topic among Christians has been whether women can hold these local church offices, specifically that of elder. Those who would say no to this are called *complementarians*, because they believe that even though God created men and women equal in essence, he also gave them distinct and different roles and responsibilities, and these complement one another. One of their main texts is 1 Timothy 2:12: "I do not permit a woman to teach or to have authority over a man." Those who would say yes are called *egalitarians,* because they believe men and women are equal in essence as well as authority. One of their main texts is Galatians 3:28: "There is neither Jew nor Gentile, neither slave nor free, nor is there male nor female, for you are all one in Christ Jesus."

INTERESTING FACT

It seems that in the first century, whereas the office of elder was mandatory for local churches, the office of deacon was not. It could be used if the priorities of the elders were threatened by material needs. However, in the twenty-first century, it seems that the office of deacon is essential due to material matters, such as church buildings and properties, financial record-keeping for nonprofit organizations, etc. Now many issues threaten the spiritual priorities of pastors and elders, and these priorities must be protected.

What Is the Significance of Baptism?

A regular part of Christian worship is the practicing of ordinances or sacraments. *Ordinance* refers generally to any kind of a rule or regulation established by an authority, and specifically, to a religious rite or ceremony. Some denominations use the term *sacrament*, meaning "something that is sacred or holy," which has the additional idea of a channel of divine grace, that is, God makes his grace available in a special way through those ceremonial practices.

Those denominations that prefer the term *ordinance* do not understand these practices to be channels of divine grace in any unusual way. Rather, they are God-given means by which Christians remind themselves of foundational truths in our faith, and believers practice them in obedience to our Savior, who has commanded us to do these things regularly.

All churches and denominations agree that baptism and the Lord's Supper are to be regularly practiced as divine ordinances.

We will consider baptism in this chapter and the Lord's Supper in chapter 36.

The importance of baptism can be seen in the example of Jesus himself being baptized by John the Baptist (Matthew 3:13–17). As a part of the Great Commission, Jesus also commanded his followers to baptize as they made disciples (Matthew 28:19). So for Christ-followers, baptism is not optional but mandatory. Luke documents that the early church was faithful to follow Jesus' command (Acts 2:38, 41; 8:12–13, 36–38; 9:18; 10:47–48). Baptism was so important to first-century Christians that there really is no such New Testament thing as an "unbaptized believer." The pattern—clearly and repeatedly—was believe and *immediately* be baptized.

The general concept of baptism is identification or association with something or someone. It was common in the Greco-Roman mystery religions, and so most Gentiles would have been familiar with it. The Jews required baptism in their conversion rituals for Gentiles, so Jews too understood the concept. There are several types of baptism in the New Testament, for example, the baptism of John the Baptist (Matthew 3:6); baptism into Moses (1 Corinthians 10:2), and baptism by the Holy Spirit (1 Corinthians 12:13). All of these have in common the idea of identification or association.

Christian (water) baptism, then, means identification or association with Jesus Christ and his gospel. In Romans 6:1–11, Paul says that Christians were baptized into Christ, but more specifically into his death, burial, and resurrection (v. 4). The point he's making is that the believer has already died, already been buried, and already been resurrected with Christ in a *spiritual* sense, and is therefore dead to sin and alive to God. So Christian baptism is best understood as an outward (physical/visible) indication of an inward (spiritual/invisible) reality; it is a means by which a believer publicly proclaims his or her faith in and identification with Christ.

Some churches do believe in what is called "baptismal regeneration," meaning that it is necessary for a person to be baptized in order to become a Christian. However, this seems to contradict the biblical teaching that we are saved not based on anything we do for God but only on what God has done for us through Jesus. Paul vehemently argued against the necessity of circumcision for salvation (Romans 3:30; 4:9–12; see also Acts 15:1–29), because that would fit into the category of human works, which have nothing to do with our salvation. Baptism would seem to fit into the same category.

Sometimes Acts 2:38 is used to support baptismal regeneration. Here Peter tells people, "Repent and be baptized, every one of you, in the name of Jesus Christ for the forgiveness of your sins." In light of all New Testament teaching regarding how to be saved by God's grace alone through our faith in Jesus Christ alone, what Peter said probably is best understood to reflect the close association between becoming a Christian and *then* being baptized (in that order). So baptism is not necessary to become a Christian but is important for someone to do who believes; it is a matter of obedience.

Who to Baptize?

Who should be baptized? Historically, there have been two answers: Some believe infants can and should be baptized, and others believe only those old enough to exercise personal faith in Christ should be baptized.

Those who practice *infant* baptism, also known as paedobaptism, argue that Christian baptism is the New Covenant equivalent of circumcision under the Abrahamic Covenant. In the Old Testament, Hebrew baby boys were circumcised and considered a part of God's covenant community—the nation of Israel. In the New Testament, under the New Covenant, baptism is the God-given means by which children are welcomed into the community of faith in Christ. This link is seen in Colossians 2:11–12.[1]

The argument is also made that household conversions and baptisms (e.g., Acts 11:14; 16:15, 31; 18:8) must have included infants. Also, Jesus received children into the kingdom of God and told his followers to do the same (Mark 10:14–16). We are to do this by means of baptism. In addition, when Peter said, "Repent and be baptized" (see above), he went on to say: "The promise is for you *and your children*" (Acts 2:38–39). This practice was taught by the early church fathers and can be documented back to the second century. It is practiced today by the Roman Catholic Church, the Episcopal Church, and Methodist, Lutheran, and Presbyterian churches.

Those who practice *believer's* baptism say there are no explicit New Testament examples of infants being baptized. The paedobaptist assumption that infants were part of household conversions is just that: an assumption; the text does not explicitly say. But there are many explicit examples of new believers being baptized, that is, those old enough to understand the gospel and make a personal decision of faith in Christ (Matthew 28:19; John 4:1–2; Acts 2:41; 8:12, 38; 9:18; 10:48; 16:14–15, 32–34; 18:8). This makes sense, because the only way to be saved is through faith, and infants are not old enough to grasp what must be understood and believed in the content of the gospel. Believer's baptism is practiced by Baptist churches, Evangelical Free churches, and many independent or nondenominational churches.

How to Baptize?

How should baptism be done? Three modes have been practiced through church history.

The practice of *sprinkling* is based on the Old Testament rituals of sprinkling with blood to cleanse from sin or disease (e.g.,

Exodus 24:6–8; Leviticus 1:11; 14:7). This mode of Christian water baptism was not regularly used until the thirteenth century.

A second mode of baptism is *pouring*, which symbolizes the coming of the Holy Spirit upon the believer (Acts 2:17–18). Drawings in the catacombs of Rome depict this practice.

The final mode of baptism is *immersion*. The argument in favor is that this is exactly what the Greek word *baptizō* means— to plunge, dip, or immerse. This mode also best illustrates the believer's spiritual death, burial, and resurrection with Christ, as described in Romans 6:3–4. Immersion seems to be the standard practice of the early church from the first century.

INTERESTING FACT

In addition to the Lord's Supper and baptism, the Roman Catholic Church also observes marriage, confirmation, holy orders, penance, and extreme unction (anointing the sick or dying) as sacraments. A few Protestant denominations observe foot washing as an ordinance.

What Is the Significance of the Lord's Supper?

The second church ordinance all Christians practice is the Lord's Supper, also known as the Lord's Table, Communion, or the Eucharist, meaning "thanksgiving." The model is the Passover meal, the Last Supper, as observed by Jesus and his disciples just before his arrest, trials, and crucifixion (Matthew 26:26–29; Mark 14:22–25; Luke 22:14–23; 1 Corinthians 11:23–26).

Jesus identified the bread with his body, which he offered as a sacrifice for sin (1 Peter 2:24), and the wine with his blood, which he shed for the forgiveness of sin (Ephesians 1:7). Elsewhere, Jesus is identified with the Passover event itself (1 Corinthians 5:7) and is called the Lamb of God (John 1:29, 36), whose blood cleanses and redeems (1 Peter 1:19).

Transubstantiation

As to the meaning of the Lord's Supper, the Roman Catholic view is called *transubstantiation*: During the Mass, when the priest consecrates the bread, it actually becomes Christ's physical body, and when he consecrates the wine, it actually becomes Christ's physical blood. This is based on John 6, where Jesus said, "I am the bread of life" (v. 35) and "Whoever eats my flesh and drinks my blood has eternal life" (v. 54). This position sometimes is called "the actual presence" view because it holds that Jesus is actually and physically present in the bread and wine of the Mass.

The Protestant reformers said this would amount to a re-sacrificing of Jesus, whereas Hebrews says his sacrifice was a once-for-all-time event (10:10–14). Also, "I am the bread" was metaphorical speech, just as when he said, "I am the vine" (John 15:1, 5), "I am the light of the world" (John 8:12; 9:5), and "I am the gate for the sheep" (John 10:7). Clearly he did not intend to imply that he is a literal, physical vine, gate, or light. Alternative views began to emerge.

Consubstantiation

The Lutheran view is called *consubstantiation* (or the real-presence or mystical-presence view). After consecration, the bread remains bread and the wine remains wine; however, the real, physical body and blood of Jesus are, as the Lutheran confessions put it, present "in, with, and under" the bread and wine. The bread and wine are *not* the body and blood of Jesus, but they do *contain* his body and blood.

Think of how a sponge does not change into water when submerged but is thoroughly infused with the water. The bread and wine are not changed into body and blood, but the body and blood of Jesus permeate the bread and wine.

Other reformers raised a concern with this view. If Jesus

ascended to heaven with his physical body, how could his physical body also be here on earth in any sense—whether through transubstantiation or consubstantiation? The physical human body can only be at one place at one time, and right now, the physical body of Jesus is in heaven.

Memorialism

Another model that emerged from the Reformation was *the memorial view,* originally argued by Ulrich Zwingli, a Swiss reformer. Memorialism focuses on the words of Jesus (Luke 22:19) and Paul (1 Corinthians 11:24–25) that the Lord's Supper is to be done "in remembrance." Paul adds that this event is a way of "proclaim[ing] the Lord's death until he comes" (v. 26).

In Old Testament times, God often gave his people a sign to help them remember a covenant, for example, the rainbow for the Noahic covenant (Genesis 9:13–16) and circumcision for the Abrahamic covenant (Genesis 17:10–14). In the same way, the Lord's Supper was to be the God-given sign by which believers remember their covenant, the new covenant, with him.

Jesus himself makes the connection between the supper and the new covenant (Luke 22:20). As such, the bread and wine neither become nor contain his *physical* body and blood; they are *symbols* that represent his body and blood, significant in that they remind participants of his sacrificial death and the covenant established as a result.

Those who hold the memorial view do not deny that Jesus is present during the celebration of the Lord's Supper. His presence, though, is spiritual, not physical, and his presence is no different than at any other time or place, since he promised *always* to be with his followers (Matthew 28:20). In memorialism, then, the Lord's Supper is an ordinance, not a sacrament, for it does not channel God's grace in any unusual way.

Spiritual Presence

A final view held by many reformers is somewhere between the Lutheran and Zwinglian convictions. This is known as the reformed view (which is a bit broad, since Luther and Zwingli also were reformers) or more specifically, *the spiritual presence view.* According to this understanding, the bread and wine neither become nor contain Christ's *physical* body and blood, but they do contain his *spiritual* body and blood. When Jesus said the bread was his body and the cup was his blood, he did not mean it literally, but he did mean the bread and wine were more than mere symbols. He was saying that when his followers practiced the supper, he would be there in a very special way, "more than" his promised presence in all other situations. The Lord is present *spiritually* at the Lord's Supper and at work *spiritually* through the eating of the bread and drinking of the wine. These, then, are means through which Christ conveys his grace to his followers, and the Lord's Supper is thus considered a sacrament.

How to Practice the Lord's Supper

Only those who have truly believed in Jesus and are trusting in him and him alone for their salvation should participate in the Lord's Supper. This as a local church practice should (respectfully) exclude unbelievers attending on that particular day. And significantly, those who partake are to be "worthy" believers.

Paul addressed this serious matter due to abuses among the Corinthian believers (1 Corinthians 11:17ff.). Those who participate in an "unworthy manner will be guilty of sinning against the body and blood of the Lord" (v. 27). Christians "ought to examine themselves before they eat of the bread and drink from the cup" (v. 28); the idea seems to be that one must scrutinize and, if needed, correct his or her motives, attitude, and comprehension of the event's significance. This is no empty ritual to be observed flippantly—we are to partake in reverence.

INTERESTING FACT

Those who uphold the sacramental aspect of the ordinances also believe there are other means by which God conveys his grace in a special way, such as through prayer and the preaching of his Word.

Is Jesus Really Coming Back?

Many people these days are thinking about the future. This was not so true until relatively recently, because in the larger scheme of things, not much was changing from century to century. In the last few hundred years, though, things have started to change, and even more recently, to change rapidly. It is difficult for us to imagine what life will be like in ten years, let alone a hundred or a thousand! So more and more people have questions like, "Where is all of this going?" or, "What does the future hold?"

The Bible has some of the answers. Nearly all Christians from the first century on have believed Jesus Christ is coming back to earth someday. Why? Because the New Testament makes it abundantly clear. His sermon known as the Olivet Discourse is about events leading up to and including his return (Matthew 24–25; Revelation 19:11–21 also describes his return).

What Does the Bible Reveal?

During the Last Supper, Jesus said,

My Father's house has many rooms; if that were not so, would I have told you that I am going there to prepare a place for you? And if I go and prepare a place for you, I will come back and take you to be with me that you also may be where I am.

John 14:2–3

At his ascension, two angels promised, "This same Jesus, who has been taken from you into heaven, will come back in the same way you have seen him go into heaven" (Acts 1:11).

The epistles often mention the second coming. Paul taught very new believers to anticipate and prepare for Christ's return. They did not always grasp the details, so he wrote to clarify matters (e.g., 1 Thessalonians 4:13–5:11; 2 Thessalonians 2:1–12) about this great event he calls the "blessed hope" (Titus 2:13).

The word *hope* here differs in meaning from how we often use it ("I *hope* I win the Publishers Clearing House Sweepstakes!"). The New Testament concept refers to a *confident* expectation of something future; you hope in something because you *know* for certain that one day it *will* be a part of your experience. Other writers also encouraged Christians to live in light of the return of Jesus (e.g., James 5:7–8; 1 Peter 1:13; 2:12; 4:7, 13; 5:1–4).

The New Testament mentions the second coming more than three hundred times. Not only is every Christian to know this wonderful reality, it also should be his or her daily longing. Jesus "will appear a second time for salvation without reference to sin, to those who eagerly await Him" (Hebrews 9:28 NASB); "Keep yourselves in the love of God, waiting anxiously for the mercy of our Lord Jesus Christ to eternal life" (Jude 21 NASB).

What Difference Should It Make?

The crucial point here is that the second coming is not just a theological truth we should know and believe; it is a certainty that should have a profound impact on how we live daily.

First, as John explains, the return of Christ should motivate us to live holy lives in anticipation of standing before our Savior.

> Dear friends, now we are children of God, and what we will be has not yet been made known. But we know that when Christ appears, we shall be like him, for we shall see him as he is. All who have this hope in him purify themselves, just as he is pure.
>
> 1 John 3:2–3

Peter, in the context of assuring that Christ is indeed coming back, says, "What kind of people ought you to be? You ought to live holy and godly lives as you look forward to the day of God and speed its coming" (2 Peter 3:11–12; see also v. 14).

Second, the return of Christ should cause us to be faithful in his absence and therefore ready for his coming, whenever it may be. At the end of the Olivet Discourse, Jesus told a series of parables to make this point. He told us to "keep watch, because you do not know on what day your Lord will come" (Matthew 24:42). The faithful servant does what his master charges him to do in the master's absence and is found doing it when his master unexpectedly returns (vv. 45–51). Jesus also said, "Look, I come like a thief! Blessed is the one who stays awake and remains clothed, so as not to go naked and be shamefully exposed" (Revelation 16:15).

Third, the hope of Christ's return is to be a comfort and encouragement to us in the present as we endure hard times. Paul corrected the Thessalonian Christians with regard to their understanding of the second coming, but after each clarification he said, "Therefore encourage one another with these words" (1 Thessalonians 4:18; see also 5:11). All the suffering on earth that believers experience needs to be seen in the perspective of what the future holds:

> Our light and momentary troubles are achieving for us an eternal glory that far outweighs them all. So we fix our eyes not on what

is seen, but on what is unseen, since what is seen is temporary, but what is unseen is eternal.

2 Corinthians 4:17–18

In other words, the unimaginably wondrous blessings Christ will bring for his people and what they will experience with him forever in eternity will make *any* suffering on this earth more than worth it. Specifically, believers who suffer through persecution for the name of Jesus are to be comforted by their hope—that is, their knowledge of the certainty—of his return:

God is just: He will pay back trouble to those who trouble you and give relief to you who are troubled, and to us as well. This will happen when the Lord Jesus is revealed from heaven in blazing fire with his powerful angels.

2 Thessalonians 1:6–7

Jesus is indeed coming back. We should believe this with great confidence. But even more so, this blessed hope should shape our thoughts, motives, attitudes, words, and actions every day. And our longing should be, "Come, Lord Jesus" (Revelation 22:20).

INTERESTING FACT

As I write this, England's William and Catherine are celebrating their first hours of marriage. Vast crowds have lined the streets, awaiting the newlywed couple's short open-carriage ride from Westminster Abbey to Buckingham Palace for just a glimpse of their future king and queen. This is a beautiful picture of what all believers should constantly, consciously, and "anxiously" look for: the coming of the King of Kings, our Lord and Savior.

When Is Jesus Coming Back?

The Bible provides some signs or indications of Christ's approaching return. Jesus himself reveals a number of these in the Olivet Discourse (specifically, Matthew 24:4–35). What makes this area of theology so difficult, however, is that prophetic statements regarding Messiah's coming to reign on earth are scattered throughout Scripture, and it is a monumental challenge to harmonize them or put together the puzzle's pieces.

Furthermore, much of the prophetic literature is in poetic form and in a genre called "apocalyptic," so whether predictions should be understood figuratively or literally is a subject of debate. As a result of these obstacles, there have been three broad views regarding the flow of events in the "end times": amillennialism, postmillennialism, and premillennialism.

The term *millennium*, from the Latin word for "thousand years," is based on the opening verses of Revelation 20, which speak of Christ reigning for a thousand years. "The millennium" basically is synonymous with the concept of "the kingdom." How does this, then, fit with the second coming?

Amillennialism

Amillennialism indicates that this view denies the millennium, that is, a literal, earthly and physical future reign of Christ. Rather, it is believed his reign began at his first coming, so he is reigning now—either on earth in the lives of believers individually and the church corporately (the majority amillennial view), or in heaven, as Christ sits at the right hand of his Father (a more recent, minority amillennial view).

Amillennialism is sometimes known as *realized eschatology*, in contrast to "futurist eschatology," because the messianic kingdom has been realized and thus is not a future reality to be anticipated. Jesus seemed to indicate this, for example, when he said, using the present tense, "The kingdom of God is in your midst [or, within you, or among you]" (Luke 17:21). This view also holds that moral and spiritual conditions will deteriorate as the time of Christ's return approaches (2 Timothy 3:1–9). When he comes, all people will be resurrected and be judged. The eternal state will then be established.

Amillennialism has largely come from the significant theological influence of the fourth-century church father Augustine, especially his book *The City of God*. The majority view through the majority of church history, it is the standard belief of the Roman Catholic and Eastern Orthodox Churches.

Amillennialism results from a more figurative or spiritual interpretation of many prophetic texts. For example, the entire book of Revelation is taken in a more figurative way, and the "thousand years" (20:1–7) refers not specifically to one thousand years but rather to a long period of time, namely, the time between Christ's first and second comings.

Postmillennialism

Like amillennialism, being based upon a more figurative interpretation of prophetic texts, postmillennialism denies any *physical* future reign of Christ *on earth*. Rather the millennium, or "kingdom," will be a very long era that is brought about as God works through the evangelistic efforts of believers on earth. *Un*like amillennialism, postmillennialism is intrinsically optimistic, holding that the gospel of Jesus Christ will be effectively proclaimed, the world will be thoroughly evangelized, and even those who do not specifically profess Jesus as Savior and Lord will be so profoundly affected by a Christian worldview that the world will be characterized by righteousness and peace.

So the kingdom is not established at Christ's first coming, but rather sometime in the flow of church history between his first and second comings. *After* this long period of the "kingdom," Jesus will return—*post*millennial. Like amillennialists, postmillennialists believe that the resurrections, the judgments, and the eternal state will then occur.

Postmillennialism, which developed in the seventeenth century, was popular thereafter due to the influence of the Enlightenment, advances in science and education, and the Industrial Revolution. But two world wars and the increasing visibility of wickedness throughout the world have led to a decline, even though the view has enjoyed a recent revival of sorts.

Another term that applies to some who hold to postmillennialism (and possibly amillennialism) is *preterism*, from the Latin word meaning "past." Generally, preterism asserts that some biblical prophecies concerning the "last days" already were fulfilled (before AD 70), implying that the kingdom is now a reality. Specifically, preterism says "last days" refers to the last days of the Mosaic covenant, or the Old Testament Law.

God verified the Law's end when he allowed the temple in Jerusalem to be destroyed in AD 70. This is what Jesus meant by "This generation will certainly not pass away until all these things have happened" (Matthew 24:34, a crucial preterist text). Prophecies regarding the "antichrist," "tribulation," and "day of the Lord" were fulfilled in the middle of the first century. Jesus Christ did return—not physically, but spiritually, and not to reign, but to judge. But most preterists do believe Jesus will return physically in the future, and then will follow the resurrection of all, the judgment of all, and the eternal state.

Order of Events

Amillennialism	Postmillennialism
1. The kingdom was established at the advent; Christ is reigning on earth through Christians or in heaven.	1. The kingdom has been or will be established on earth by the church sometime between the advent and the second coming.
2. Wickedness will increase as time goes on.	2. Righteousness will increase as time goes on.

3. Christ will return to earth.
4. The righteous and the wicked will be resurrected and judged.
5. The eternal state will be established.

Premillennialism

Premillennialism is the view that Jesus will yet return physically and that he himself will establish his kingdom and reign on earth for a thousand years—a millennium. Unlike the other two views, this one results from interpreting prophetic texts much more literally (while still seeking to handle the elements of poetic literature and figures of speech responsibly).

For example, premillennialism is based on a literal understanding of the Abrahamic covenant, in which God promised Abraham many descendants (today called Jews) and a land for them to dwell in forever (then known as Canaan or Palestine, and today Israel; Genesis 12:1–3; 13:14–17), and the Davidic covenant, in which God promised David many descendants and that among those would be an eternal throne or kingdom, a continuation of David's reign (2 Samuel 7:4–17). It maintains that God's promises in these covenants have *not* yet been fulfilled—they are *not* fulfilled in a *spiritual* sense in the church today (as amillennialism/postmillennialism say) but will be, literally and fully, in the millennium, along with the promises of the new covenant, announced in Jeremiah 31, and inaugurated by Christ's death and resurrection. This view interprets Revelation literally (while recognizing the nature of apocalyptic literature and the presence of figures of speech).

Premillennialism was the generally accepted view during the church's first three centuries, up until the time of Augustine. Its modern-era resurgence began during the nineteenth century.

In chapter 39, we will look at the flow of future events from a premillennialist perspective in a bit more detail.

FUN FACT

Jesus Christ is returning in judgment *today*! Or so a certain preacher said would happen this evening (May 21, 2011, as I write)—specifically, 6:00 PM around the world. Obviously, since you are reading this, he was wrong. By no means was he the first to forecast the date (*or* the hour) of the second coming; all such "foretellings" have proven false. The problem is that Jesus himself said no one knows the time of his return except his Father (Matthew 24:36). As we have seen, soon thereafter he said, "Keep watch, because you do not know on what day your Lord will come" (v. 42). And again, the application is: Be ready!

What Will Happen
When Jesus Comes Back?

The end-time events according to amillennialism and post-millennialism are relatively simple. In chapter 38, we saw that premillennialism says Christ will return visibly and physically in the future and reign on earth for a thousand years. Premillennialism's flow of events is somewhat more complex.

Tribulation and Rapture

Within premillennialism, there are several views on the tribulation and the rapture. The tribulation is understood to be a period of seven years, based on Daniel's vision of seventy "sevens" (Daniel 9:20–27). This will be a time of great suffering and cataclysm on earth, including the pouring out of God's wrath upon sinful humanity. Described in 1 Thessalonians 4:13–18, the term *rapture* comes from the Latin rendering of the Greek word in verse 17, translated into English as "caught up." The event is the catching up of resurrected Christians, and of Christians still living on earth when Jesus returns, to meet him in the air.

There are three predominant sub-views within premillennialism. Some believe Christians will be raptured *before* the tribulation and will spend those seven years in heaven until Jesus returns to earth to reign for a thousand years; this is known as the *pre-tribulation-rapture* view. Its adherents maintain that the rapture is "imminent"—it could occur at any time. The rapture and the return of Christ to reign on earth are separated by seven years.

Others believe Christians will endure the entire seven-year period of the tribulation and be raptured at its end—the *post-tribulation-rapture* view, wherein the rapture and Christ's return to reign on earth are one event.

A few others believe Christians will remain on earth for some time within the seven-year tribulation and then will be raptured for the duration. Some of these believe the rapture will occur specifically at the tribulation's midpoint—the *mid*tribulation-rapture view; others believe the rapture will occur sometime during the tribulation, but specifically preceding the outpouring of God's wrath upon sinful humanity—the *pre-wrath*-rapture view.

Order of Events

Pretribulationism	Midtribulationism and Pre-Wrath Rapture	Posttribulationism
1. The church will be raptured and taken to heaven.	1. The tribulation will begin on earth.	1. The tribulation will take place on earth.
2. The tribulation will take place on earth.	2. The church will be raptured at the tribulation's midpoint *or* before God begins to pour out his wrath.	2. The church will endure the tribulation.
3. Christ will return to earth with the church.	3. Christ will return to earth with the church.	3. Christ will return, rapture the church, and proceed to earth.

Otherwise, premillennialists generally agree on the events as follows:

4. Christ will return from heaven with an army (Revelation 19:11–14). Those on earth who are gathered together to fight against him will be defeated and killed (19:15–21).
5. Satan will be bound for a thousand years and thrown into the abyss (20:1–3).
6. The righteous dead will be resurrected to inherit the kingdom. This includes, for example, Old Testament saints. (More on the end-time resurrections and judgments below.)
7. Jesus will establish his kingdom and will reign for a thousand years. The saints will reign with him (20:4–6).
8. At the thousand years' end, Satan will be released to lead one more futile rebellion against Jesus. God will quickly defeat him (20:7–10).
9. The unrighteous dead—all people of all time whom God has not accepted and forgiven—will be resurrected, judged, and sent to their eternal destiny apart from him (20:11–15).
10. Eternity will be ushered in with the new heaven, new earth, and New Jerusalem (21; we will look at these in more depth in chapter 40).

Resurrections and Judgments

The Old Testament is nearly silent regarding the concept of resurrection, though Isaiah 26:9 and Daniel 12:2 give several clear statements. The New Testament clearly and repeatedly refers to resurrection. In contrast to the Sadducees, who denied it, Jesus affirmed its reality (Matthew 22:29–32) and identified the concept with himself (John 11:25–26).

Apostolic proclamation of the gospel often referred to Christ's resurrection (e.g., Acts 2:31). After Paul's arrest in Jerusalem, he claimed to be on trial because of his hope in the resurrection from the dead (23:6). He also wrote the major New Testament statement on the resurrection in 1 Corinthians 15, where he says, "If the dead are not raised, then Christ has not been raised either. And if Christ has not been raised, your faith is futile; you are still in your sins" (vv. 16–17). Truly, the resurrection is one of the believer's great hopes (2 Corinthians 5:2–3).

All people who have ever lived will be resurrected for the purpose of judgment (John 5:27–30). God has judged sin in the past (e.g., the flood, Sodom and Gomorrah), but all of these historical judgments only anticipate the future and final divine judgment of sin and sinners and of the righteous.

Jesus referred to this in his Olivet Discourse in terms of the separation of the sheep and the goats (righteous and unrighteous; Matthew 25:31–46). The sheep will inherit the kingdom and eternal life, but the goats will be sent away into eternal fire and punishment. Jesus specifically will be the final judge of all.

The judgment of believers will be at the "judgment seat of Christ" (2 Corinthians 5:10; also Romans 14:10–12; 1 Corinthians 3:10–15). Pretribulationism holds that this will take place in heaven after the rapture and during the tribulation on earth. Posttribulationism maintains that this, along with the judgment of Old Testament saints, will take place at the beginning of Christ's millennial reign.

The works of believers will be judged to determine reward or loss of reward (1 Corinthians 3:15). These rewards are called "crowns" (2 Timothy 4:8; James 1:12; 1 Peter 5:4). Since judgment of believers' sin has already fallen on Jesus (Romans 3:21–26; 8:1), this is not an issue in the final judgment (1 Corinthians 3:15). One aspect to be judged is faithfulness with regard to what has been entrusted in Christ's absence (Matthew 25:14–30; Luke 19:11–27; 1 Corinthians 4:2). Another aspect is the "heart" of the believer (1 Corinthians 4:5). It is important to God not only that we do right and good things but also that we do them in right and good ways—with proper attitudes and motives.

The judgment of the unrighteous will take place at the "great white throne" (see Revelation 20:11–15). The basis will be their sinful deeds generally, but specifically their unwillingness to honor and glorify God (Romans 1:18–23), and, if they have heard the gospel, to believe in Jesus Christ as Savior (John 5:22–29). Their fate will be the "lake of fire," also known as the "second death" (Revelation 20:14–15).

Satan and the demons will also be judged at this time (2 Peter 2:4; Jude 6–7; Revelation 20:10). Interestingly, Christians will participate in this judgment (1 Corinthians 6:3). Finally, the present heavens and earth will be destroyed (2 Peter 3:10) to prepare the way for the new heavens and earth, which will be a part of the eternal state (Revelation 21:1).

INTERESTING FACT

It seems the population will grow during the millennium. Resurrected saints cannot reproduce (Matthew 22:30), but believers who survive the tribulation and enter Christ's kingdom in mortal bodies can. Their children will need to believe in King Jesus in order to be saved. Apparently many will not believe (amazingly!), and they will make up Satan's final rebellion army (Revelation 20:8).

What Will Heaven Be Like?

Future resurrections will result in final judgments, and final judgments will confirm final, everlasting destinies for both the righteous and the unrighteous.

Tragically, the unrighteous will spend eternity separated from God in hell, being punished for their sins and unbelief. Most references to hell are in the Synoptic Gospels (Matthew, Mark, and Luke) and are from Jesus himself (e.g., Matthew 5:21–30; Mark 9:43–48; Luke 12:5). He described hell as a terrible reality of suffering and despair, and therefore, his clear warning was to do whatever is necessary to avoid it.

The English word *hell* is used to translate two Greek words: *hades* and *gehenna*. *Hades* seems to be where the unrighteous are sent to be punished while they wait for their final judgment (e.g., the rich man of Luke 16:19–31); it is *temporary*. However, according to Revelation 20:14, death and Hades will be thrown into the lake of fire in the final judgment. So it seems the lake of fire is the more specific way to refer to the *eternal* destiny of the unrighteous (v. 15).

The Greek word *gehenna* seems to be the New Testament reference to this eternal destiny. The term is derived from the Valley of Hinnom, adjacent to Jerusalem. It was a place of Old Testament idol worship that became the city's garbage dump, where the bodies of executed criminals would be thrown. So the imagery is of a pit of constant burning, smoke, fire, and destruction, and this is exactly how the New Testament describes the eternal dwelling of the wicked: It is a "blazing furnace, where there will be weeping and gnashing of teeth" (Matthew 13:42; see also 8:12; 25:41; Revelation 21:8). Regardless of whether these terms and descriptions are to be taken literally (punishment will consist of actual fire) or metaphorically (punishment will be terrible and painful, like that of fire), hell is a place of unimaginably horrible suffering.

Some do not believe the unrighteous will suffer in punishment *forever.* According to the view called *annihilationism,* God will eventually annihilate the unrighteous; they will cease to exist after a period of punishment. The arguments used for annihilation include the following:

First, because God is love, he will not be able to tolerate the never-ending, conscious anguish of those who bear his image.

Second, the finite sins committed by the unrighteous do not deserve infinite or everlasting punishment.

Third, the biblical terms for this punishment include "destruction" and "fire," both of which imply an end of existence.

Some who hold this view also adhere to "conditional immortality," the belief that no one is inherently immortal; rather, God gives immortality as a gift of salvation to the righteous. So the unrighteous were never immortal and will therefore cease to exist at some point.

The traditional view, however, is that the punishment of the unrighteous will indeed be unending. The strongest biblical argument for this and against annihilationism is Matthew 25:46, where Jesus said, "Then [the unrighteous] will go away to eternal punishment, but the righteous to eternal life." The word *eternal* is applied to both destinies. If the righteous enjoy life that lasts forever (which the Bible clearly, repeatedly affirms), then it seems necessary to conclude that the punishment of the unrighteous will likewise be forever. Other texts also speak of this punishment as being eternal (Matthew 18:8; 25:41; Mark 9:48; 2 Thessalonians 1:9; Revelation 14:11; 20:10).

Scripture does seem to establish eternal punishment for the unrighteous but also seems to imply that there will be degrees of punishment, the very wicked being punished more severely than the lesser wicked. This would be the purpose of judging the unrighteous according to their works (Matthew 16:27; Revelation 20:12–13). For example, those who have heard the gospel and rejected it will be punished more severely than those who have never heard the gospel (an implication of Matthew 11:20–24).

Whereas the eternal destiny of the unrighteous will be separation from God forever, the righteous will be in God's presence forever. The term *heaven* has been traditionally associated with the eternal dwelling of God's people. In addition to being used of physical reality (earth's atmosphere and outer space), it also refers to a spiritual realm, the dwelling of God and angels. This is where Jesus went after his ascension (Luke 22:69; Acts 7:55; Romans 8:34) and where the righteous go after physical death to await their resurrection (Luke 23:43; 2 Corinthians 5:8; Philippians 1:23; 1 Thessalonians 4:14).

However, after the resurrection of the righteous and in eternity, their dwelling seems to be the new heaven and the new earth (Isaiah 65:17; 66:22; 2 Peter 3:13; Revelation 21), which will replace the old heaven and earth after the final judgment (2 Peter 3:10). The new heaven and earth will probably be a renewal (rather than replacement) of the original creation, but with all the destructive effects of sin and the curse removed (Romans 8:19–21; Revelation 22:3).

God declared his original creation to be "very good" (Genesis 1:31), and his work bringing about the new heaven and earth will restore his creation to that state. It will be "paradise" (Revelation 2:7), like the garden of Eden. In fact, Revelation (21–22) picks up concepts from Genesis 1–3, indicating that God does complete what he had intended to accomplish in his work of creation (see the "Fun Fact" at the end of chapter 20 in *Understanding Your Bible in 15 Minutes a Day*).

The eternal state will also include the New Jerusalem. John wrote, "I saw the Holy City, the new Jerusalem, coming down out of heaven from God, prepared as a bride beautifully dressed for her husband" (Revelation 21:2; more in vv. 10–27). It is immense—fourteen hundred *miles* in three dimensions. It is brilliant with the glory of God, constructed of precious metals and jewels. It will have no temple, because God will be the temple, and there will be no sun, because his glory will supply the light. This will be a place in which death, tears, sorrow, and pain are excluded. It will be a place of holiness, life, service (22:3), fulfillment, and joy—*perfection*. This is the inheritance of God's people (21:7), where they will reign with him forever (22:5). Some believe the New Jerusalem is what brings heaven and earth together forever.

The real significance of all this was revealed to John in this way:

> God's dwelling place is now among the people, and he will dwell with them. They will be his people, and God himself will be with them and be their God.
>
> 21:3

This was God's intention from the beginning, as demonstrated by his fellowship with Adam and Eve in the garden of Eden

(Genesis 3:8). But the entrance of sin into creation resulted in a separation between holy God and sinful humanity (3:23–24).

God's desire to dwell among his people was also demonstrated in the tabernacle (Exodus 25:8). The prophets reminded them of his intention to dwell among them (Ezekiel 37:26–28). He now dwells among his people by dwelling within them through his Holy Spirit (1 Corinthians 3:16; 2 Corinthians 6:16). And his intention will be fully realized in the eternal state. This is the greatest salvation benefit of all—to enjoy a perfect and unhindered relationship with God.

God's people *"will see his face"* (Revelation 22:4)! They will experience the reality of David's words in Psalm 16:11:

> In Your presence is fullness of joy;
> In Your right hand there are pleasures forever.
>
> NASB

Is there *any* wonder why the book of Revelation ends with the plea, *"Come, Lord Jesus"* (22:20)?

INTERESTING SUGGESTION

I will end this chapter in the same way I ended chapter 6: It is my belief that eternity will be an unending theology class. Every day of eternity, God will reveal another aspect of his infinitely glorious being for the joy of his people. I still can't wait!

Epilogue

You have merely dangled your toes in the deep ocean of the amazing things of God. I hope you have enjoyed this book and benefited from it. But even more so, I hope you are desperate for more and will continue to go deeper into the truth and explore its mysteries for the rest of your life. And I hope you too look forward to the ongoing theology class called *eternity*.

Notes

Introduction

1. The word *proper* indicates a narrower use of the term *theology*, since all of these categories fit the broader term.

Chapter 1: What Is Theology?

1. Charles Ryrie, *Basic Theology* (Chicago: Moody, 1986), 9.

2. This idea is developed well in Stanley Grenz and Roger Olson, *Who Needs Theology? An Invitation to the Study of God* (Downers Grove, IL: InterVarsity, 1996).

Chapter 3: How Do We Know the Bible Is the Word of God?

1. Parts of this chapter appeared previously in Daryl Aaron, *Understanding Your Bible in 15 Minutes a Day* (Minneapolis: Bethany House, 2012), chapter 25.

2. For more, see ibid., chapter 27.

3. In this book, all italics in quoted Scripture are the author's, used for emphasis.

Chapter 4: What Are the Implications of the Bible Being the Word of God?

1. Parts of this chapter appeared previously in Daryl Aaron, *Understanding Your Bible in 15 Minutes a Day*, chap. 28.

2. In the Old Testament, the Hebrew word *elohim* often refers to God himself. In Psalm 82, however, it is used in verses 1 and 6 of human rulers or judges under the absolute rule and judgment of God himself (see also Exodus 22:8–9; Psalm 58:1). The point Jesus is making in John 10:34–36 is that if human rulers can be called "gods," what is wrong with Jesus claiming to be God's Son, as he had been set apart and sent by God himself?

3. Quoted by Harold Lindsell, *The Battle for the Bible* (Grand Rapids: Zondervan, 1976), 54, 57.

4. For example, Jack B. Rogers and Donald K. McKim, *The Authority and Interpretation of the Bible: An Historical Approach* (San Francisco: Harper & Row, 1979).

5. The ICBI no longer exists, but the "Chicago Statement" is easily found online.

6. Lindsell, 57.

7. Ibid., 54.

Chapter 5: What Are Other Implications of the Bible Being God's Word?

1. Parts of this chapter appeared previously in Daryl Aaron, *Understanding Your Bible in 15 Minutes a Day,* chap. 28.

Chapter 6: What Characteristics of God Make Him Unique?

1. Not all theologians agree on which attributes fit which category.

Chapter 7: What Other Characteristics of God Make Him Unique?

1. The theological systems known as Arminianism and Calvinism will be discussed in more depth in chapter 11.

2. Technically, this is a *communicable* attribute because humans have wisdom as well, or at least should have. I deal with it here because it is so closely associated with God's knowledge.

3. An excellent survey of this very important biblical theme can be found in John Piper, *Desiring God* (Portland, OR: Multnomah, 1986, 1996, 2003), 308–321.

4. This would be a communicable attribute, since we can and should be holy people.

5. Piper, *Desiring God,* 42.

Chapter 9: What Does It Mean That God Is a Trinity?

1. Alister E. McGrath, *Christian Theology: An Introduction,* 4th ed. (Oxford: Blackwell, 2007), 249.

Chapter 12: What Are Angels and Demons?

1. This is debated. Some interpreters believe these are not references to Satan but rather to ancient human kings of Babylon and Tyre.

Chapter 13: What Does It Mean to Be Human?

1. The following three categories are developed by Millard J. Erickson in *Christian Theology,* 2nd ed. (Grand Rapids: Baker, 1998), 520–529.

Chapter 14: Do Humans Have Parts?

1. Erickson, *Christian Theology,* 554.

2. Wayne Grudem, *Systematic Theology* (Grand Rapids: Zondervan, 1994), 472–483.

Chapter 22: What Does It Mean to Say That Jesus Is Lord?

1. Duane Litfin, *Conceiving the Christian College* (Grand Rapids: Eerdmans, 2004). He develops this idea throughout chapter 3.

2. Ibid., 47.

Chapter 26: What Is the Basis of Salvation?

1. In all these texts, the NIV translates the Greek word for *propitiation* as *atonement* or *sacrifice of atonement*. Unfortunately, this obscures the term's specific idea of "turning away wrath."

Chapter 28: Did Jesus Die for Everyone?

1. D. A. Carson does an excellent job of presenting this position in *The Difficult Doctrine of the Love of God* (Wheaton, IL: Crossway, 2000), 73–79.

Chapter 35: What Is the Significance of Baptism?

1. Those who uphold believer's baptism argue that these verses refer to *spiritual* circumcision and *spiritual* baptism, not physical circumcision or physical (water) baptism.

Daryl Aaron earned his MA at the University of Texas–Dallas, his ThM at Dallas Theological Seminary, his DMin at Bethel Theological Seminary, and his PhD at the Graduate Theological Foundation. He spent fourteen years in pastoral ministry and now teaches at Northwestern College, where he is Professor of Biblical and Theological Studies. Dr. Aaron lives in Mounds View, Minnesota, with his wife, Marilyn. They have one daughter, Kimberly, who recently completed her master's program and will join her (very proud) father on the faculty of Northwestern College teaching Spanish.

More User-Friendly Guides in 15 Minutes a Day

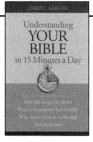

Whether you're a beginner or a seasoned reader, the Bible can be overwhelming at times. The short, digestible readings in this book dispel myths about where the Bible came from, what it is about, and why it matters. With its easy-to-navigate topical structure, this guide offers quick and clear answers to your most important questions about the bestselling book in history.

Understanding Your Bible in 15 Minutes a Day
by Daryl Aaron

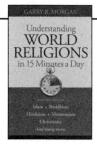

In an increasingly global world, what once seemed like the religions of faraway lands are now practiced by families next door. In this accessible guide, a cross-cultural expert gives quick, clear, real-world answers to questions about the beliefs and practices of dozens of religions, including Islam, Buddhism, Hinduism, and Christianity.

Understanding World Religions in 15 Minutes a Day
by Garry R. Morgan

⬧BETHANYHOUSE

Stay up-to-date on your favorite books and authors with our *free* e-newsletters. Sign up today at bethanyhouse.com.

 Find us on Facebook.